COMFORT & JOY

RAVINDER BHOGAL

IRRESISTIBLE

PLEASURES

FROM A

VEGETARIAN

KITCHEN

COMFORT
& JOY

BLOOMSBURY PUBLISHING
LONDON · OXFORD · NEW YORK · NEW DELHI · SYDNEY

For Nadeem, my own comfort and joy

BLOOMSBURY PUBLISHING
Bloomsbury Publishing Plc
50 Bedford Square, London, WC1B 3DP, UK
29 Earlsfort Terrace, Dublin 2, Ireland

BLOOMSBURY, BLOOMSBURY PUBLISHING
and the Diana logo are trademarks of
Bloomsbury Publishing Plc

First published in Great Britain 2023

Text © Ravinder Bhogal, 2023
Photographs © Kristin Perers, 2023
Author photograph on page 272
© Rahil Ahmad, 2023

Ravinder Bhogal, Kristin Perers and Rahil
Ahmad have asserted their right under the
Copyright, Designs and Patents Act, 1988,
to be identified as Author and Photographers
of this work

A catalogue record for this book is available
from the British Library

Library of Congress Cataloguing-in-
Publication data has been applied for

ISBN: HB: 978-1-5266-5537-0;
eBook: 978-1-5266-5536-3

2 4 6 8 10 9 7 5 3 1

Project editor: Laura Nickoll
Designer (interior pages): Sandra Zellmer
Designer (cover): Carmen Balit
Photographer: Kristin Perers
Food stylists: Joss Herd and Hattie Arnold
Prop stylist: Tabitha Hawkins
Indexer: Vanessa Bird

Printed and bound in China by C&C Offset
Printing Ltd

To find out more about our authors and books
visit www.bloomsbury.com and sign up for
our newsletters

COMFORT & JOY

A kitchen well stocked with vegetables, pulses and grains is brimming with the potential for joy. It promises abundance – a multitude of reliable, economical and delicious options. Even undervalued staples such as a dense head of cabbage or celeriac – strange, warty and impenetrable – have always been a boon to me in my kitchen because I was brought up in a culture where vegetarianism is the norm. I inherited my vegetable literacy and the knack for cooking vibrant, inventive food without relying on the safety blankets of meat and fish from my long lineage of plant-eating ancestors, many of whom remained in agile health well into their ninth decades.

We already know that a diet made up largely of fruits, vegetables, beans, legumes, grains and nuts is healthier for us *and* our planet, but my purpose is not to preach or to be militant and forceful about dietary choices. Instead, this book is a celebration of the vegetarian option; engaging dishes that are miles away both in flavour and charisma from the dour school of vegetable cookery that has been prevalent in the

West where plants are traditionally relegated to supporting-role status. Over the last decade there has already been a cultural shift towards vegetable-forward eating, but there is still room for us to lavish plants with the kind of care, culinary sorcery, creativity and surprise that we might bring to a steak or a chop.

Vegetables are the soul of the kitchen – they can stand on their own and jangle with flavour without the need for lard, animal flesh or strange proteins masquerading as meat. This book presents dishes that you'll gravitate towards, ones that bring comfort and joy and that incidentally happen to be meat free too. Comfort food means different things to different people, but for me comfort and joy go hand in hand – feel-good, life-enhancing dishes that nurture, nourish and lift your mood; food you never, ever get tired of eating; and meals that bring equilibrium when the world seems fraught. Importantly they should transmit a bounty of love and warm sentiment while still eliciting oohs and aahs. And of course, if eating a diet that is mostly plants improves our wellbeing *and* the health of our broader world even in a small way, then that's a cause for joy. From fortifying dhals upholstered with bright homemade pickles, tangles of slippery noodles dressed in a dazzling array of seasonings and condiments and sweet fruit bringing razzle dazzle to savoury dishes, this verdant, globally inspired collection of recipes is enough to tempt even the most unrepentant carnivores.

The vegetarian kitchen offers endless opportunities for play. The wide spectrum of cereals, beans and lentils, roots, shoots, bulbs, herbs and leaves crossed with the myriad of diverse culinary cultures to draw on for inspiration means there is always a bounty of good things to eat, even when the landscape of your larder seems meagre. Vegetables are versatile too. Carrots, beetroots and turnips, for example, do very well when they are thinly shaved and quick-pickled with white wine vinegar and a few aromatics such as black peppercorns, cinnamon and cloves. Like mellow sweet potatoes, Jerusalem artichokes, swedes and parsnips, they can also be roasted till burnished golden and caramelised or boiled and mashed into silken purees lavished with cream, butter and the addition of something feisty like fresh ginger, turmeric or even citrus and fragrant spices like ground cardamom and grated nutmeg. For the cook, there is great reward in teasing out a miracle of flavour from the most underrated ingredients, be it a dowdy cauliflower or a humble tin of chickpeas.

Crave-able vegetarian food relies on balance, textural contrast, fresh ingredients and a well-stocked global larder. Indian, Asian and Middle Eastern cuisines in particular have a knack of reinvigorating the usual suspects found lurking in the vegetable drawer with zesty condiments, complex spice mixes and umami sauces and pastes. But my connection with vegetables and vegetarian eating is a deeply personal and nostalgic one. It goes back my roots when I myself was a seedling, well over 30 years ago on my grandfather's *shaamba*[1] in Nairobi.

The plot was not grand – it was a mass of red earth – merely a scrap of cultivated land, penned in by a boundary of a few wispy saplings, but to me it was Edenic. It was lush and alive, full of the melodic croon of birds and the hum of insects in every handful of soil; busy centipedes, enterprising ground beetles, dandy praying mantises and leopard-printed ladybirds. On yellowed heat-hazed afternoons the opportunistic and wily cats that belonged to no one gave chase to a rainbow haze of butterflies and then collapsed – defeated – in patches of wan sunlight. Sometimes a young goat broke loose from its herd and dropped in for a snack of sweet, tender shoots.

Aged five, I loved to play hide and seek in the foliage that was then as tall as me. It was here, munching sweet peas set in their pods like precious malachite pearls under an ever-blue sky, that I felt free – liberated from the rigid code of conduct and chaste manners my mother expected her daughters to observe. She certainly did not approve of me returning home as I often did rumpled – the alluvial red soil clinging to my new white leather sandals, its rust stain on my starched broderie-anglaise smock.

My grandfather had moved to Kenya from India as a young man seeking an escape from a provincial life. Things were more difficult than he'd anticipated – he was disorientated by language barriers, the racial divide in a country that was then still a British colony and extreme solitude. Making money was challenging too, and he'd been dealt the fuzzy end of the lollipop in a few business deals. Yet he was happy – he'd traded security for independence and adventure and was better off on unfamiliar territory than the stifling provinces of Punjab.

Bhaji[2] died when I was very young, but I have remained in awe of him – of his generosity and deeply entrenched belief in the Sikh ideology of *seva*[3]. He was hardworking and full of Punjabi verve – a pioneer who left everything he knew to take a voyage in the dark. He embodied for me all that was good and pure in the world – he was the exemplary man. When *Bhaji* first arrived in Nairobi, he saved some money and purchased an unloved plot. But he persevered with it, working it day and night, laying down seed, manure and love, until the generous Great Rift Valley rain baptised both him and the land, and it blossomed into fertility like a radiant girl unfurling into womanhood. He shared everything he grew, donating the bounty to neighbours and friends, to the Mama Ngina orphanage or to rural medical camps. He reminded me often that the easiest way to be helpful was simply by feeding people.

If I close my eyes, I can still picture him standing in the middle of the vegetation – letting the tender fronds tickle his splayed palms, cutting fodder with powerful musical swipes of the *fanga*[4]. He'd smile broadly as he pulled out onions from the earth and held them close as though they were precious nuggets of gold. His weatherworn face protruded from under the white cloud of his turban, his forehead marked with deep crevices of determination, wisdom behind the twitching curtain of his eyelashes. He had an intimate relationship with the land. The gush of love that ebbed from him into the landscape came from the deep wounds of someone who had known harsh, uncertain times. Several times a day he lifted his eyes skyward and uttered '*Waheguru*'[5] with gratitude at the abundance providence had provided. He spent his days weeding, watering and propagating until the sun came back around and his shadow spread like a blossoming tree over the crumbling whitewashed wall.

In Kenya, meat was eaten rarely. Instead our daily meals were songs of praise devoted to the seasonal homegrown fruits and vegetables from our allotment, or those purchased from the *mama mbogas*[6] who grew astonishingly fresh varietals of every kind of seed, bean and pod in their smallholdings, harvesting them every morning and then peddling them door to door in the city suburbs. Until I arrived in England aged seven I had never eaten a supermarket vegetable. I found myself pining for our Nairobi kitchen with the pistachio terrazzo floor and its walls of peeling paint in eggshell hues – for the mind-boggling variety of vegetable dishes cooked on its hissing and clanking old stove. Iron-rich *sukuma*[7] sautéed simply with chopped onions, roasted cumin and buxom tomatoes plucked straight off the vine, weighty aubergines that were charred on the *jiko*[8] until they collapsed in on themselves to make smoky *baingan bhartha*[9] and *vadiya* – sundried ground lentil dumplings reconstituted in a feisty turmeric-infused broth.

In those early sepia-tinged days of homesickness and anguished longing, I meditated often on the small pleasures of the *shaamba* – picking fresh green chickpeas and putting them in my pocket as a snack for later, splitting an unripe mango sprinkled with chilli, salt and sugar with my sisters, or sinking my milk teeth into a sun-ripened pink guava. In our modest English kitchen, my mother consoled me with the vegetarian

dishes that signified the comforts of my childhood idyll; bitter gourds
stuffed with peanut masala paste, cubes of cassava – boiled, then fried
till supernaturally crisp before being tossed in chilli, salt and lime juice
– or vegetable *pakoras* buoyantly bobbing about in a soothing primrose-
yellow buttermilk soup – every morsel a remembrance of home. Even
now, when the world feels like a wilderness, I find safety, memories of
my grandfather and the place I come from contained in the veg box.
Unfurling onions from their silky, clinging jackets, or gently opening
an unblemished courgette flower can feel extraordinary – they have
stoically held their own against the elements, pests and blight – their
presence in our kitchens is life affirming. I flutter with gratitude at the
fruit bowl and understand, now, why my grandfather found refuge and
restoration in the *shaamba*.

In my kitchen both at home and at work, I aspire to push vegetables
to the fore and create nourishing vegetarian food that transports
the people I am feeding into a soft-focus cocoon where you spoon
something soporific into your mouth and forget the world exists
for anything but your pleasure – each vegetable, fruit or pulse deftly
cooked and seasoned considerately with something that tastes
like love. In the chapters ahead you'll find recipes to serve every
occasion; from a quick weeknight supper where you might want
the reassuring chew of noodles or a simple bowl of dhal to those
nights where you might be hosting a grown-up dinner party. There
are recipes for delicious dips on which I could happily live alone,
all manner of pleasing crisp fried things like fritters and croquetas,
breads and pancakes to really get your teeth into, delicious bolstering
dhals and soothing soups, fragrant curries and stews, hefty salads
packed with fistfuls of good things, vegetable sides that steal the
show, rice, pasta, noodles and grains, pickles and condiments to
enliven and enhance every plate and finally puddings to tickle that
sweet tooth. These recipes explore vegetarian food in all its glorious,
abundant manifestations.

I have come to understand that there are many layers to the comfort
and joy of vegetables – landscape, soil, allotments, life force, sunshine,
imperfectly perfect produce, bees, memory, home, taste, scent – and
sharing it all somehow makes everything taste better. I learnt this from
my grandfather who lived for this joy, for these small comforts.

1   Allotment
2   Term of endearment for grandfather
3   Community service
4   Machete
5   Wonderful God
6   Female vegetable sellers
7   Collard greens
8   Outdoor coal stove
9   Aubergine mash

1
DIPS, SALSAS, HUMMUS AND RELISHES

TAKE A DIP

The best TV snacks are the ones you can't stop eating. And while there are lots of crisps, chips and cookies that fit the bill, most of them make me feel sort of blah once the binge is done. Over the years of being hooked to latticework storylines, plot twists and cliff hangers, I have developed quite the binge-watch snack repertoire.

There are some rules for optimal snackability – your snackage must have texture, taste and accessibility – that is, it shouldn't require too much culinary faculty or cutlery. This is why dips like hummus, salsa and guacamole have had such runaway success. It also helps that many favourite dips are built around an indispensible ingredient that you are always likely to have in your kitchen – chickpeas, tomatoes, avocados. The best dips are vivacious and bursting with contrasting flavour – spiky heat from chilli, earthiness from spices or vivid acidity from lemon or vinegar to counter the voluptuous fattiness of olive oil.

It is likely that your first encounter with a dip came in the form of hummus. Its tantalizing combination of chickpeas, lemon juice, olive oil and tahini may have roots in the Middle East, but it is universally loved – I myself am such a tahini fiend that I must be half woman, half hummus. I love it and convenience too much not to buy it ready made, but the top-tier dreamy stuff – uniformly creamy and buttery – is always homemade. In my kitchen it gets scooped straight from the blender, all light and fluffy, into a shallow bowl – the craters of milky surface marbled with golden rivulets of my best olive oil. I may sprinkle over za'atar, perfumed Aleppo pepper, paprika or something pickled and sharp. My preferred vehicle for shovelling it into my mouth is pita bread, speckled and puffy from the oven, thick enough to hold up against the weight of a generous helping or, if I am being health conscious, whatever I can forage from my veg box depending on the season – heirloom tomatoes, cigars made from rolled-up herbs, baby cucumbers, sugar snap peas, radishes or wedges of fennel or lettuce. Other times I just eat it straight from the pot with a spoon.

Dips go beyond film fodder – they can make a sophisticated offering at social gatherings where you can simply place a platter or a bowl in the middle of a table with raw vegetables or spread a dip generously onto rounds of grilled baguette. They're the perfect accompaniment to drinks and, once they are made, it's all self-service. And while social gatherings like dinner parties are always about the company, I find sharing dips is an ice breaker of sorts – they are conduits for lively, engaged and lingering conversation so long as you mind your manners and don't double dip.

I'll admit that I don't mind a dip over a proper dinner too. On particularly harried days, I usually make a hearty dip like my aubergine bhartha and serve it alongside a few different types of crackers or chips, raw vegetables and little piles of herbs. Sometimes I'll layer dips like my hot corn and cheese dip drizzled with jalapeno relish. However you eat them, these homemade dips will make you question why you ever bothered with any of the pedestrian store-bought stuff.

PEA, PRESERVED LEMON *and* MINT DIP *with* RADISH SALSA *and* FETA

One of my earliest memories is of gobbling raw sweet peas straight out of the pod in my grandfather's *shaamba*. They tend to get overlooked as a vegetable, but they are allowed to shine unobstructed in this simple zesty dip. It can conveniently be made with fresh or frozen peas and is equally lovely piled on toast with soft-boiled eggs for breakfast.

———

To make the radish salsa, combine the radishes with the sugar and vinegar in a bowl, season with salt and set aside.

Bring a large pan of salted water to a roaring boil, add the peas and cook for 3 minutes or until tender. Drain well, then add to a blender along with the garlic, preserved lemon and mint leaves and blend. Slowly pour in the oil and blend till smooth then season to taste with salt and pepper.

Smooth the dip over a serving platter and drizzle over some more olive oil. Spoon over the radishes and crumble over the feta. Scatter over some extra mint leaves and serve with bread and crudités.

· 500g peas (fresh or frozen)
· 2 fat garlic cloves, finely chopped
· Rind of 1 small preserved lemon, finely chopped
· Handful of mint leaves, chopped, plus extra leaves to garnish
· 3 tbsp extra virgin olive oil, plus extra for drizzling
· 100g good-quality feta cheese, crumbled
· Sea salt and black pepper

FOR THE RADISH SALSA
· 10 radishes, thinly sliced
· ½ tsp caster sugar
· 1 tsp apple cider vinegar

SOUTH INDIAN
BEETROOT *and* COCONUT DIP
with CURRY LEAVES

This vibrant magenta dip brings an interesting friction to sweet earthy beetroots with a South Indian spice tempering. You can eat this as a component part of a larger South Indian meal or serve it with shards of paratha or poppadums. If you don't want to make parathas, buy them frozen – they are available in most supermarkets now – and stash them in your freezer.

————

Heat the rapeseed oil in a large frying pan over medium heat, add the grated beetroot and sauté for 8–10 minutes until it becomes a little tender.

In the meantime, make the coconut paste. Blitz together the mustard seeds, sesame seeds and cumin seeds in a blender then add the cashews, coconut, ginger and chilli along with a little water and blitz until you have a smooth paste.

Add the coconut paste to the beetroot and cook for a further 5–8 minutes over low-medium heat until the raw ginger and chilli have become fragrant. Let the mixture cool, then blitz in the blender again and mix through the yoghurt. Season with salt to taste and stir in the caster sugar and lime juice. Pour into a serving bowl and set aside.

To make the tempering, heat the coconut oil in a small frying pan over high heat. When hot, sprinkle in the mustard seeds. As soon as they sputter and pop, add the asafoetida, curry leaves and Kashmiri chilli, pour over the beetroot dip and serve.

· Drizzle of rapeseed oil
· 4 medium beetroots, peeled and grated
· 200g natural or vegan coconut yoghurt, beaten well
· 1 tsp caster sugar
· Juice of 1 lime
· Sea salt

FOR THE COCONUT PASTE
· ½ tsp brown mustard seeds
· 1 tsp white sesame seeds, toasted
· ½ tsp cumin seeds, toasted
· 8 cashew nuts, toasted
· 100g fresh or frozen grated coconut, defrosted
· 1 tbsp peeled and grated ginger
· 1 green chilli

FOR THE TEMPERING
· 2 tbsp coconut oil or rapeseed oil
· 2 tsp brown mustard seeds
· Pinch of asafoetida
· 15 fresh curry leaves
· 1 dried Kashmiri chilli, broken up

NORI-SALATA
TOASTS

The pleasures of holidays are fleeting, but the memories and the influence of the foods and flavours far outlast the plane ticket home. A few years ago, I travelled to Crete where there were savage landscapes, transparent waters, quiet coves and unhurried villages to be discovered, but for me the legendary food was the bona fide tourist attraction. Full disclosure – I've always had a fetish for taramasalata. A smear of this dusky pink Greek spread transports me to happy times at tavernas overlooking the Aegean, drinking ouzo with ice. This version is vegan so of course it contains none of the traditional carp roe, but, thanks to the briny flavour of the nori, it still tastes like something that was plucked from the sea.

––––––––––

Finely grind the toasted nori in a blender. Transfer to a bowl, clean out the blender and then combine the tofu, bread, onion and lemon juice in it and process until smooth. While the motor is still running, gradually add the oil and process until combined. Season to taste with salt and pepper and three-quarters of the ground nori and mix again. Transfer to a bowl, cover and chill until required.

To serve, spread generously onto toast and top with a sprinkle of nori and togarashi or chilli flakes. Serve with lemon wedges for squeezing over.

· 8 sheets toasted nori
· 200g silken tofu, patted dry and broken up
· 100g crustless white bread, soaked in water then drained and squeezed
· 1 white onion, finely grated
· Juice of 1 lemon
· 150ml extra virgin olive oil
· Sea salt and black pepper

TO SERVE
· 8 thin slices of sourdough toast
· Togarashi or a few dried chilli flakes
· Lemon wedges

BURNT COURGETTE *and* CARDAMOM DIP *with* CRISPY CAPERS

This recipe is a perfect way to make the most of the glut of late summer courgettes. While it's similar to an aubergine baba ghanoush, it's a lighter, silkier spread perfumed with a subtle whisper of green cardamom. The fried capers add a wonderful piquancy.

————

Preheat the oven to 230°C/Fan 210°C/Gas Mark 8 or turn up a grill to its fiercest setting. Place the courgettes on a baking tray and roast for 45 minutes in the oven or under the grill, turning them frequently until they are blackened and charred all over. Let them cool down.

When the courgettes are cool enough to handle, cut them in half lengthways and, using a spoon, scoop out the meltingly soft flesh and place it in a sieve to drain for 15 minutes. Discard the burnt skins. In a large bowl, whisk together the olive oil, tahini, garlic, cardamom seeds and lemon juice. Roughly mash the courgette flesh and fold through the tahini base. Season well with salt and pepper then mix through the mint.

Peel the whole lemon with a peeler lengthways, making sure not to put too much pressure on the peeler – you don't want the bitter white pith. Then, using a sharp knife, thinly slice each peel widthways to give you thin, short shards of lemon zest.

Heat the rapeseed oil in a pan over medium-high heat. Once hot, add the capers and fry for 1 minute until they are crisp and puffed up. Add the lemon zest shards and fry briefly then scatter over the dip, drizzle with some extra virgin olive oil and serve.

· 6 large courgettes
· 60ml olive oil
· 40g tahini
· 2 garlic cloves, crushed
· Seeds from 10 green cardamom
  pods, toasted and crushed
· Juice of 1 lemon
· Handful of mint, finely chopped
· Sea salt and black pepper
· Extra virgin olive oil, to serve

FOR THE CRISPY CAPERS
· 1 lemon
· 2 tbsp rapeseed oil
· 2 tbsp capers, rinsed and drained

HOT CHEESE *and* CORN DIP *with* JALAPENO RELISH

This sunshine-yellow dip is inspired by one I ate at a hole-in-the-wall Tex-Mex restaurant in New York many years ago. Everything else I ate was pretty forgettable, but I was taken in by its deeply savoury cheesiness – every pert nugget of corn swathed in molten goodness. I am a freak for heat, so I drizzle over a punchy jalapeno relish for a fresh contrast to all the creaminess.

———

For the jalapeno relish, put all the ingredients in a blender and blend together until smooth. Set aside until needed.

Clean out the blender and puree half the sweetcorn kernels with 75ml of water until it is very smooth and then, if you want a really creamy dip, pass through a sieve and discard the remaining solids. You can leave out this step if you prefer a chunkier dip.

Heat the oil in a shallow casserole dish over medium heat and, once hot, sprinkle in the cumin seeds, add the cinnamon stick and sizzle for 30 seconds or until fragrant. Next, add the spring onions, garlic, chilli and lemon zest and fry over low heat until fragrant and softened. Tip in the whole sweetcorn kernels and fry for about 10 minutes. Finally, add the pureed sweetcorn and cook until it is all bubbling. Sprinkle in the cheese, spoon in the sour cream and stir until it is molten and glossy. Season well. To serve, transfer to a bowl, drizzle over the jalapeno relish, scatter with the finely chopped coriander and stud the dip with a few pickled jalapenos. Enjoy scooping the hot corn.

- 450g frozen sweetcorn kernels, defrosted
- 2 tbsp rapeseed oil
- ½ tsp cumin seeds
- 1 cinnamon stick
- 5 spring onions, thinly sliced (including green parts)
- 3 garlic cloves, finely chopped
- 1 long red chilli, thinly sliced on the diagonal
- Zest of 1 lemon
- 225g mature Cheddar, grated
- 50g sour cream
- Sea salt and black pepper

FOR THE JALAPENO RELISH
- 2 fresh green jalapeno chillies
- Juice of 1 lime
- 50ml olive oil
- 1 spring onion, thinly sliced
- 1 small garlic clove
- Large handful of coriander, roughly chopped

TO SERVE
- 2 tbsp finely chopped coriander
- A few pickled jalapenos

CARROT *and* GOAT'S YOGHURT DIP
with FENNEL,
CARAWAY *and* HAZELNUTS

The addition of anything lactic – from yoghurt to cheese – brings both a fatty voluptuousness and tang to dips. Here, goat's curd adds a welcome contrasting sharpness to this otherwise earthy carrot dip. If you can't find goat's milk yoghurt, simply whizz together 50g of soft goat's cheese with 125g regular yoghurt in a blender till smooth.

———

Preheat the oven to 200°C/Fan 180°C/Gas Mark 6.

Lay the carrots and unpeeled garlic cloves in a single layer on an oven tray, scatter with the cumin seeds, pul biber and thyme and drizzle with 80ml of the olive oil. Season with salt and pepper and roast for 1 hour until golden and very tender. Remove from the oven and leave to cool to room temperature.

Squeeze the garlic cloves from their skins, discard the thyme, then transfer the contents of the tray to a blender along with the yoghurt, lemon zest and juice and blend until smooth. While the motor is running, add the remaining oil in a steady stream.

Toast the fennel and caraway seeds in a frying pan over low heat for a minute or two until fragrant and then empty into a bowl. Put the carrot dip in a serving bowl and serve topped with a drizzle of olive oil, the toasted spices and chopped toasted hazelnuts.

- 1kg carrots, peeled and sliced into thick discs
- 1 head of garlic, unpeeled but cloves separated
- 1 tsp cumin seeds
- 1 tsp Turkish pepper flakes (pul biber) or ½ tsp dried chilli flakes
- A few sprigs of fresh thyme
- 180ml extra virgin olive oil, plus extra for drizzling
- 150g goat's milk yoghurt
- Zest and juice of 2 lemons
- 1 tsp fennel seeds
- 1 tsp caraway seeds
- 50g toasted hazelnuts, roughly chopped
- Sea salt and black pepper

WHIPPED FETA *with* CONFIT TOMATOES

Cold, salty feta topped with tomatoes warmed in olive oil that has been studded with aromatics until they are bursting, gooey and have a heightened sweetness are the perfect topping for hunks of grilled bread. These tomatoes are also pretty perfect tossed together with pasta or gnocchi which I just throw straight into the roasting tin before tossing and eating.

———

Preheat the oven to 180°C/Fan 160°C/Gas Mark 4.

Cut some of the larger tomatoes in half and leave some whole and place in a roasting tin along with the garlic and lemon peel. Season with salt and pepper and sprinkle over the caster sugar, coriander seeds, chilli flakes and oregano and then drizzle over the olive oil. Bake for 40 minutes until the tomatoes are bursting and fragrant. Cool down slightly, then discard the garlic and lemon peel.

In the meantime, put the feta cheese into a food processor along with the lemon juice and whizz until smooth and creamy. Transfer to a bowl and stir in the yoghurt.

Put the whipped feta in a serving bowl and top with the warm tomatoes. Serve with slices of toasted sourdough bread.

· 400g mixed cherry tomatoes
· 5 garlic cloves, peeled and bruised
· 3 thin strips of lemon peel
· ½ tsp caster sugar
· 1 tsp coriander seeds
· ¼ tsp dried chilli flakes
· 4 sprigs of oregano
· 60ml extra virgin olive oil
· Sea salt and black pepper

FOR THE WHIPPED FETA
· 200g good-quality feta cheese
· Juice of ½ lemon
· 100g thick Greek yoghurt

AVOCADO, EDAMAME *and* YUZU DIP *with* FURUKAKE

Everybody loves guacamole and, until I ate this dip, I thought it was the best thing to come out of avocado. The buttery lusciousness of avocado needs acidity and yuzu juice brings a surprising perfumed sweetness. If you can't get hold of yuzu, mix together the juice of a lemon and a clementine to mimic its sweet, sherbet sharpness. The edamame beans add a chunky texture to the dip, making it more pleasantly substantial on your chip.

———

This couldn't be simpler. Blitz the avocados together with the edamame beans, ginger, soy sauce and sesame oil in a food processor until you have a chunky textured dip. Stir in the yuzu juice to taste. Serve topped with furukake.

· 4 very ripe avocados, stoned and peeled
· 300g frozen edamame beans, defrosted
· 1 tsp peeled and grated ginger
· 2 tsp light soy sauce
· A few drops of toasted sesame oil
· Yuzu juice, to taste (or mix the juice of 1 lemon and 1 clementine)
· 2 tbsp furukake (see page 226)

GREEN LENTIL HUMMUS
with CRISPY SHALLOTS

Hummus can be made with almost any pulse. I love making it with green lentils which, unlike dried chickpeas, don't require any presoaking. The addition of crispy shallots makes this dip moreish. A plate of it along with some pita bread, olives, boiled eggs and shaamba pickles (page 220) makes for a perfect, simple lunch.

———————

First, make the crispy shallots. Fill a deep, heavy-based saucepan with a depth of 6–8cm oil and put over medium heat until it reaches 180°C (if you don't have a digital probe thermometer, a cube of bread added to the pan will turn golden in 20 seconds at this temperature). Line a plate with kitchen paper and set aside. Scatter the shallots into the oil and fry, turning and moving them around in the pan frequently until dark golden brown. Remove from the oil with a slotted spoon and drain well on the kitchen paper. Season with a little salt and set aside to cool.

To make the dip, combine the stock, green lentils, cinnamon, cardamom pod and bay leaf in a saucepan and bring to the boil, then cover and simmer over low heat, stirring occasionally, until the lentils are tender – this will take about 45 minutes. Uncover the pan and boil the lentils over high heat until most of the liquid has evaporated. Discard the bay leaf, cinnamon and cardamom pod and let the lentils cool slightly.

Put the cooked lentils in a food processor. Add the garlic, tahini, olive oil and lemon juice and puree until smooth. Stir in the parsley, season with salt, cumin seeds and chilli powder to taste, mix, then spoon into a serving bowl. Drizzle over extra olive oil as desired and scatter over the pine nuts and crispy shallots.

- 800ml vegetable stock
- 175g green lentils
- 1 cinnamon stick
- 1 black cardamom pod, bruised
- 1 bay leaf
- 3 fat garlic cloves, finely chopped
- 60g tahini
- 60ml extra virgin olive oil, plus extra for drizzling
- Juice of 1 lemon
- Handful of flat-leaf parsley, finely chopped
- 1 tsp cumin seeds, toasted and finely ground
- ½ tsp red chilli powder
- Handful of toasted pine nuts
- Sea salt

FOR THE CRISPY SHALLOTS
- Rapeseed oil, for deep frying
- 2 banana shallots, sliced into very thin rings

2
FRIES, FRITTERS, CROQUETAS AND BHAJIS

BAPTISM OF THE FRYER

In the depths of hot oil in my mother's ancient deep-frying pan is a city marked by past conquerors. A samosa, a kachori, pakoda or jalebi are all reminders of our lively history, our culturally rich heritage and prosperous past. Every culture has their fried-food specialties, and, although I am probably biased, I think Indians are unparalleled in their ability to produce spicy, moreish little morsels fried to golden, crisp perfection.

Whether it's rounds of thin potatoes laced in a fragile turmeric-tinged chickpea (gram) flour batter or flaky ghee-enriched pastries generously stuffed with spicy lentils, it is impossible to eat just one. It's important these snacks are eaten immediately – still hissing with oil. That's when they are at their best, especially when dipped in fresh and bright coriander or tamarind chutney or with just a squeeze of lime.

While deep frying at home may seem daunting, Indian home cooks like my mother are experts at it. When the doorbell rings, she whips out her *kadhai* – an ancient thick, deep circular cooking pot with steep slanting sides not dissimilar to a wok. She fills it with a litre or so of rapeseed or groundnut oil and lets it heat on the stove while she deftly chops vegetables and makes a batter to fry pakoras to accompany a hot, welcoming cup of masala chai. One of my earliest memories is of watching her in the outdoor kitchen in our courtyard in Kenya piping

chickpea (gram) flour noodles into a sizzling cauldron of hot oil with
a brass *sev sancha* – a type of churros press. Watching her frying was
mesmerising and she faced the spitting oil with a kind of flamboyant
fearlessness and ease – something that comes from a lifetime of practice.
Even now, aged almost 80, she can nonchalantly whip up several
varieties of snack that are all perfectly golden and ethereally crunchy.

Small, bite-sized fried nibbles are wonderful accompanied by a drink
as a prelude to a meal. In India these vary regionally – from plump
samosas humming with chilli and cumin in Delhi to curry-leaf-scented
lentil vadas in Kerala. In Tuscany, I ate delicate fried courgette flowers
and breaded, stuffed olives, while in Sicily I indulged in arancine (fried
rice balls) and panelle (gram flour fritters served sandwiched in bread).
In Spain, I singed my eager tongue on steaming béchamel oozing from
croquetas, and I dream of visiting the temples of tempura in Japan
where delicious things are masterfully fried till they have an off-the-
Richter crunch.

I won't say this sort of frying is altogether easy or without challenges.
To the inexperienced, hot oil can seem terrifying and you will probably
approach it with anxious caution the first time, but, as you gain
confidence, the rules of fried perfection will become instinctual. You'll
delight in edges crisping, your nose will be fine-tuned to the aromatic
olfactory experience of perfectly cooked batter and, if you don't have a
thermostat or an electric fryer, you'll become proficient at regulating the
cooking temperature manually. As you master the technique, you'll be
able to do it undaunted. Is it worth the fuss or the mess? Eat a French fry
– crisp on the outside and fluffy on the inside, a perfect stick of potato
pleasure – and you will agree wholeheartedly, yes!

OKRA FRIES *with*
CURRY LEAF MAYONNAISE

People often have strong negative feelings about okra, citing its sliminess as the cause for their aversion, yet it remains popular across India, Africa and the Middle East. I have to admit that I am quite fond of its gelatinous texture, which is wonderful for thickening stews and curries, but buttermilked and fried like this you will end up with a crisp texture that is as addictive as regular potato fries with none of the viscous ooze.

––––––––––

To make the mayonnaise, begin by making the curry leaf oil. Heat the oil in a heavy-based saucepan till it's very hot then scatter in the mustard seeds. As soon as they pop, take the pan off the heat and add the asafoetida, curry leaves and chillies. Let it infuse for a minimum of 3 hours – the longer the better. Strain and discard the solids.

In a food processor, whizz together the lemon juice and egg yolks, then gradually add the curry leaf oil in a thin stream until thick and emulsified. Season to taste and refrigerate till needed.

Now for the okra fries. Trim the thick, capped ends of the okra and slice lengthways in half. Pop all the sliced okra in a bowl with the buttermilk and set aside for about 10 minutes. In the meantime, mix together the flour, cornmeal, seasoning and cayenne pepper in a shallow bowl.

Heat the rapeseed oil in a deep, heavy-based saucepan (no more than half full) to 180°C – if you don't have a thermometer, you will know the oil is ready when a cube of bread added to the pan turns golden in 20 seconds. Line a plate with kitchen paper. Dredge the buttermilked okra through the flour mix, shake off excess flour and deep fry in small batches for 3–4 minutes till golden, tender and very crisp. Drain well and place on kitchen paper. Season with chaat masala and serve with a few wedges of lime and the curry leaf mayo.

· 200g okra
· 200g buttermilk
· 125g plain flour
· 115g stone-ground yellow cornmeal or polenta
· 1 tsp sea salt
· ½ tsp freshly ground black pepper
· 1 tsp cayenne pepper
· Rapeseed oil, for deep frying
· Chaat masala, to season
· Lime wedges, to serve

FOR THE CURRY LEAF MAYONNAISE
· 175ml rapeseed oil
· 1 heaped tsp brown mustard seeds
· Pinch of asafoetida
· 15 fresh curry leaves
· 2 dried Kashmiri chillies, broken up
· 1½ tbsp lemon juice
· 2 egg yolks

CRISP KALE
CHAAT

'Chaat' is a category of Indian snacks that has an enormous but unquantified number of delicious manifestations. The word 'chaat' literally translates as 'lick' and it is true that any good one will leave you wanting to lap up the remnants on your plate. Chaats are not polite food – they are messy and often funky, served with chutneys laced with sulphurous but addictive kala namak or black salt. Their glory lies in their dishevelment and imperfections and this is what makes them so enduringly enticing and approachable. They are a flavour party – one you are always invited to – they are never dull, and they encourage inventiveness and improvisation. I have seen many adapted versions of chaat all over the world made ingeniously with local ingredients. What unifies each unique chaat is the tangle of blistering heat, mouth-puckering tang, addictive sweetness and lush herbaceousness.

This one is a version of a popular chaat often made with spinach – I have used more robust kale because, where chaat is concerned, there are no rules and reinvention is cool!

————————

- Rapeseed oil, for deep frying
- 150g chickpea (gram) flour
- 50g rice flour or cornflour
- 1 tsp cumin seeds
- ½ tsp chilli powder
- ½ tsp coriander seeds, roughly crushed
- ½ tsp ajwain or carom seeds
- ½ tsp turmeric
- 2 tbsp finely chopped coriander
- ½ tsp sea salt
- 275ml ice-cold sparkling water
- 200g kale, tough ribs removed
- Chaat masala, for sprinkling

TO SERVE
- 150g natural yoghurt, whisked
- Green Coriander and Mint Chutney (page 224)
- Date and Tamarind Chutney (page 226)

TO TOP THE CHAAT
- 4 tbsp nylon sev or puffed rice
- 1 tomato, finely chopped
- 1 small red onion, finely chopped
- Seeds from ½ pomegranate
- Handful of coriander, finely chopped
- 1 red chilli, thinly sliced on the diagonal

To make the kale chaat, heat the oil in a deep, heavy-based saucepan (no more than half full) to 180°C – if you don't have a thermometer, you will know the oil is ready when a cube of bread added to the pan turns golden in 20 seconds. Line a plate with kitchen paper.

Combine the flours, spices and fresh coriander in a large mixing bowl. Season with the salt then whisk in the sparkling water a little at a time until you have a batter the consistency of a crêpe batter. Dip the kale leaves in the batter, let the excess run off back into the bowl, and deep fry in the hot oil in small batches for 2–3 minutes until golden and very crisp. Remove with a slotted spoon, drain on the lined plate and sprinkle with chaat masala.

To serve, place the fried kale leaves on a serving platter and drizzle each one with yoghurt and the two chutneys, then top with the nylon sev, tomato, onion, pomegranate seeds, coriander and red chilli. Serve immediately for maximum crunchiness!

PEA KOFTA SCOTCH EGGS *with* SAFFRON YOGHURT

44

Peas are startlingly beautiful – I am wild about their emerald colour, like something out of Oz, their fairytale association with princesses and most of all their sweeter-than-sweet essence. When I was a child my father would bring home a sack of locally grown peas sourced from Nairobi's bustling City Market. My mother would sit me on a little stool in the courtyard and get me shelling what seemed like an insurmountable mountain of them. Some contained crawling caterpillars which made me squeal! Once podded they were ground up and mixed with earthy spices, made into little 'meatballs' and deep fried.

The blend of spices here somehow magically enhances the sweetness of the peas. We ate these koftas as they were, dipped in ketchup or sometimes immersed in a light curry. Here I have created a hybrid of my mother's Indian recipe and my British heritage. A softly boiled quail egg is cocooned in the pea kofta mix rather than sausage farce, and they are served with saffron yoghurt – it's immigrant food at its culture-bridging best.

———

- 12 quail eggs
- 700g fresh peas, shelled
- 1 banana shallot, very finely chopped
- 2.5cm piece of ginger, finely grated
- 3 garlic cloves, finely chopped
- Large handful of coriander, finely chopped
- 1 tsp ground cinnamon
- 2 tsp toasted cumin seeds, roughly crushed
- 2 tsp toasted coriander seeds, roughly crushed
- 2 green chillies, finely chopped
- Large handful of mint, finely chopped
- 1 heaped tbsp chickpea (gram) flour
- Plain flour, for coating
- 2 eggs, beaten
- 500g panko breadcrumbs
- Groundnut oil, for deep frying
- Za'atar or dukkah, to serve

FOR THE SAFFRON YOGHURT
- Fat pinch of saffron strands, roughly crushed
- 2 tbsp warm water
- 250g Greek yoghurt
- 1 garlic clove, finely chopped
- Sea salt

To make the saffron yoghurt, steep the saffron in the water for 5 minutes, then stir the saffron and water into the yoghurt along with the garlic and salt to taste. Refrigerate until required.

Bring a pan of water to the boil. Carefully lower the quail eggs into the water and simmer for exactly 2 minutes and 5 seconds. Remove with a slotted spoon and put in ice-cold water to stop them cooking any further. This should give you a lovely runny yolk. Peel and set aside.

Blitz the shelled peas in a blender till they are a coarsely ground. Tip into a mixing bowl and stir in the shallot, ginger and garlic, coriander, dried spices, chillies, mint and chickpea (gram) flour to bind. Divide the mixture into 12 equal portions.

Put some plain flour, beaten eggs and panko breadcrumbs into 3 separate shallow bowls. Wrap each egg with a portion of the pea

46

mixture – the easiest way to do this is by rolling it into a ball and flattening it into a circle large enough to wrap around the egg. Press the edges together to seal, being careful not to squash the delicate egg inside. You may find this easier to do with wet hands.

Once all the eggs have been wrapped in the pea farce, roll them in flour, then beaten egg and then the breadcrumbs. Place on a baking sheet and put them in the freezer for 5 minutes to harden slightly.

Heat the oil in a deep, heavy-based saucepan (no more than half full) to 180°C – if you don't have a thermometer, you will know the oil is ready when a cube of bread added to the pan turns golden in 20 seconds. Line a plate with kitchen paper. Deep fry the eggs in small batches for 3 minutes, being careful not to overcrowd the pan, until golden and crisp. Cut in half to serve along with the saffron yoghurt and a scattering of za'atar or dukkah.

KENYAN MARU POTATO BHAJIAS *with* TAMARIND *and* TOMATO CHUTNEY

When I was five years old and growing up in Kenya, the windows seemed as large as doors. In the rainy seasons, my cousin and I would climb into the window nooks and watch the huge raindrops lash against the polished concrete floor in the courtyard. How we longed to splish-splash in the gigantic puddles – but instead we were confined indoors which we protested was unfair and booooring – our pleas fell on deaf ears! Even the paper boats we launched out of the windows to set sail on uncertain waters had limited amusement value. Thank goodness then for rainy weather teatime snacks. These were hot, comforting and more than likely deep fried. Our favourite was Maru bhajia, the namesake of the Kenyan Indian immigrant who apparently first created them. These are irresistible thin rounds of potato, coated in a gently spiced chickpea (gram) flour batter and fried to a crisp. To this day, if it begins to drizzle outside, I have an almost Pavlovian response and crave a plate of these. They are best served straight out of the fryer along with the essential salsa-like chutney and cups of steaming chai.

———

To make the chutney, simply put all the ingredients in the blender and blitz into a coarse salsa. Season to taste and refrigerate until required.

To make the bhajia, in a large bowl, mix together the flours, spices, ginger, garlic, chilli, coriander and salt. Combine well then add the potatoes, massage over the flour and set aside for 15 minutes. You won't need to add any water as the potatoes will release liquid that will create a coating that clings to them. If it seems dry after 15 minutes, add a tablespoon or so of water – it shouldn't need more than that.

Heat the oil in a deep, heavy-based saucepan (no more than half full) to 180°C – if you don't have a thermometer, you will know the oil is ready when a cube of bread added to the pan turns golden in 20 seconds. Line a plate with kitchen paper. Lift the potatoes out of the batter, making sure they are well coated and deep fry in small batches for 4–5 minutes till golden, tender and very crisp. Drain well on kitchen paper and serve hot with the cold chutney.

· 125g chickpea (gram) flour
· 40g rice flour or cornflour
· ½ tsp ground turmeric
· ½ tsp red chilli powder
· 1 tsp cumin seeds
· ¾ tsp ajwain or carom seeds
· 1 tsp dried mango powder (amchur) – optional
· 1 tbsp peeled and grated ginger
· 2 garlic cloves, finely chopped
· 1 small green chilli, very finely chopped
· 2 tbsp very finely chopped coriander
· 1 tsp sea salt
· 4 Desiree potatoes (about 800g), peeled and sliced very thinly (preferably on a mandoline)
· Rapeseed oil, for deep frying

FOR THE CHUTNEY
· 2 tomatoes, skinned and roughly chopped
· 1 small carrot, peeled and roughly chopped
· 1 small Persian cucumber, roughly chopped
· Handful of coriander, roughly chopped
· 1 tsp toasted cumin seeds, coarsely ground
· 1 tsp chaat masala
· 1 tsp soft brown sugar or grated jaggery
· 2 tbsp tamarind paste
· Sea salt and black pepper

AVOCADO ALOO CHAAT

Potato skins are a sort of no-frills plate of food that's easy to take or leave, but a kind of next-level alchemy happens when they are introduced to the tangy, spicy flavours of an Indian bhel puri. These ones are a tantalising riot of flavours and textures, including crisp noodles (nylon sev) – outrageously crunchy little noodles made from chickpea (gram) flour – cooling avocado and coconut chutney, fragrant coriander and thrilling hot, sweet and sour date and tamarind chutney. It's a sort of Bollywood potato party on a plate.

———————

Preheat the oven to 220°C/Fan 200°C/Gas Mark 7. Rub the potatoes with salt and oil, wrap in foil and bake in the oven for about 45 minutes or until tender.

Once the potatoes are cool enough to handle, cut them in half lengthways. Use a spoon to scoop out the middles, leaving a 2cm border around the potato to keep the skins sturdy for filling later. Reserve the interior of the potatoes to use later, trying not to break the flesh of the potato too much: the skins need to remain whole as these will be cooked again and then filled. Set the skins aside.

To make the filling, crumble the cooled potato interiors into a bowl and mix with the drained chickpeas, pomegranate seeds, onion and coriander. Season with the lime juice, chaat masala, chilli powder, cumin and some salt and pepper. Mix through the date and tamarind chutney and set aside.

Heat the oil in a deep, heavy-based saucepan (no more than half full) to 180°C – if you don't have a thermometer, you will know the oil is ready when a cube of bread added to the pan turns golden in 20 seconds. Line a plate with kitchen paper. Deep fry the potato skins in the oil for 5 minutes until golden brown and crisp. Drain on kitchen paper then fill with the chickpea mixture. Drizzle with date and tamarind chutney, avocado and coconut chutney and garnish with the nylon sev, pomegranate seeds and coriander. Serve immediately.

· 4 medium baking potatoes
· Sea salt
· Rapeseed oil for deep frying, plus extra for oiling

FOR THE FILLING
· 1 × 400g tin kala channa (black chickpeas), rinsed and drained
· Seeds from 1 small pomegranate (reserve a few for garnishing)
· 1 red onion, very finely chopped
· 3 tbsp finely chopped coriander
· Juice of 1 lime
· 1 heaped tsp chaat masala
· ½ tsp red chilli powder
· 1 tsp cumin seeds, coarsely ground
· Sea salt and black pepper
· 2 tbsp Date and Tamarind Chutney (page 226)

TO TOP
· Date and Tamarind Chutney (page 226)
· Avocado and Coconut Chutney (page 225)
· 8 tbsp nylon sev
· A few pomegranate seeds
· Handful of coriander leaves

SWEETCORN, LEMONGRASS *and* LIME LEAF FRITTERS

Why restrict corn to the cob when you can turn it into these delicious fritters? These nuggets of deep-fried joy, fragrant with lemongrass and zesty lime leaves, are a version of the little snacks I scarfed at a restaurant in Indonesia. They were so delicious that I ordered them twice. The batter is made of whole corn kernels and corn that is blitzed in a food processor and plopped by the spoonful into hot oil to make a fritter that is soft and fluffy in the centre and crisp around the edges.

———

Blitz half the sweetcorn kernels in a food processor. Turn out into a mixing bowl then stir in the whole kernels, spring onions, ginger, lemongrass, garlic, lime leaves, chilli, coriander, basil, coriander seeds and soy sauce and mix. Fold in the rice flour and baking powder. Add a little water to make a thick, spoonable batter consistency.

Heat the oil in a deep, heavy-based saucepan (no more than half full) to 180°C – if you don't have a thermometer, you will know the oil is ready when a cube of bread added to the pan turns golden in 20 seconds. Line a plate with kitchen paper. Deep fry a few tablespoonfuls of the mixture for 3–4 minutes or until crisp and dark golden. Remove with a slotted spoon and drain on the kitchen paper and repeat with the rest of the mixture. Serve hot with chilli and black vinegar dipping sauce.

- 400g frozen sweetcorn kernels, defrosted
- 3 spring onions, finely chopped (including green parts)
- 2.5cm piece of ginger, peeled and finely grated
- 2 lemongrass stalks, white parts only, very finely chopped
- 2 garlic cloves, finely chopped
- 6 lime leaves, tough stems removed and leaves finely chopped
- 1 red chilli, finely chopped
- 2 heaped tbsp finely chopped coriander
- Handful of Thai basil leaves, thinly sliced
- 1 tsp coriander seeds, toasted and crushed
- 1 tbsp light soy sauce
- 100g rice flour
- 1 tsp baking powder
- Rapeseed oil, for deep frying
- Chilli and Black Vinegar Dipping Sauce (page 225), to serve

LENTIL *and* PEANUT VADAS *with* QUICK COCONUT CHUTNEY

When it comes to yoga, I am always enthusiastic but to say my practice needs work is an understatement – I am more sleeping than downward dog. On a trip to Kerala a few years ago, I found myself in a punishing yoga class. In a sea of agile yogis, in the middle of an awkward posture, I caught the eye of a kindred spirit who was struggling just as much as I was. We struck up a friendship and decided to skip the next class. She suggested we went in search of Keralan street food instead – a girl after my own heart. This recipe is inspired by the supernaturally crisp lentil fritters we ate at a roadside shack. It's a great snack to serve as a nibble with drinks, as they do in the toddy shops of southern India. There is nirvana to be found in every bite.

Soak the channa dhal in cold water for 2 hours.

To make the coconut chutney, mix together the yoghurt, coconut, sugar and lime juice in a bowl and season with salt and pepper.

Now make the tempering. Heat the rapeseed oil in a frying pan over high heat, add the dhal and fry for a minute or so until pale golden. Scatter in the mustard seeds. As soon as they pop, add the asafoetida, Kashmiri chilli and curry leaves. Pour the contents of pan over the yoghurt and stir. Refrigerate till required.

Drain the channa dhal and then grind in a food processor to a coarse paste. Add the onion, peanuts, chillies, ginger, spices, herbs, coconut, chickpea (gram) flour and salt to taste, then shape into little patties.

Heat the oil in a deep, heavy-based saucepan (no more than half full) to 180°C – if you don't have a thermometer, you will know the oil is ready when a cube of bread added to the pan turns golden in 20 seconds. Line a plate with kitchen paper. Deep fry the patties, a few at a time, for 3–4 minutes till crisp and dark golden then remove with a slotted spoon and drain on kitchen paper. Serve hot with the coconut chutney.

- 200g channa dhal (split Bengal gram)
- 1 red onion, finely chopped
- 200g skinned peanuts, coarsely chopped
- 2 green chillies, finely chopped
- Thumb of ginger, peeled and grated
- 1 tsp toasted fennel seeds, coarsely crushed
- 1 tsp toasted coriander seeds, coarsely crushed
- ½ tsp coarsely ground cinnamon
- Pinch of asafoetida
- Large handful of coriander, finely chopped
- 20 fresh curry leaves, roughly chopped
- 4 tbsp fresh or frozen grated coconut, defrosted
- 4 tbsp chickpea (gram) flour
- Rapeseed oil, for deep frying
- Sea salt

FOR THE QUICK COCONUT CHUTNEY
- 250g vegan coconut yoghurt
- 100g unsweetened desiccated coconut
- 1 tsp caster sugar
- Juice of ½ lime
- Sea salt and black pepper

FOR THE TEMPERING
- 2 tbsp rapeseed oil
- 1 tbsp urid dhal (split, skinned black gram)
- 1 tsp brown mustard seeds
- Pinch of asafoetida
- 1 dried red Kashmiri chilli, split
- 20 fresh curry leaves

SESAME TOFU TOASTS

These delicious morsels are based on the classic Chinese restaurant starter – prawn toasts. Their success relies on texture more than anything – the bounce of minced prawns and crunchy fried bread and sesame seeds. I have swapped out the prawns for extra-firm tofu which will give you a similar texture, but it needs a good amount of flavour, so season well and be liberal with the aromatics like ginger, chilli, spring onions and sesame oil. I have coated these in panko breadcrumbs as well as sesame seeds for extra crispiness. Feel free to double coat them in breadcrumbs – i.e., dip in egg followed by breadcrumbs and then repeat. You will end up with almighty crunch!

Blitz the tofu in a food processor until you have a coarse paste then empty into a bowl. Add the spring onions, garlic, ginger, chilli flakes, soy sauce, sesame oil, salt (to taste) and cornflour and mix well. Spread the mixture onto the bread, cut off the crusts and cut each piece in half diagonally. Mix together the panko breadcrumbs and sesame seeds in a shallow bowl. Brush the tops and sides of each piece of bread with beaten egg, then press into the breadcrumbs to coat. Rest in the fridge for 10–15 minutes to firm up.

Heat the oil in a deep-fat fryer or in a deep, heavy-based saucepan (no more than half full) to 180°C – if you don't have a thermometer, you will know the oil is ready when a cube of bread added to the pan turns golden in 20 seconds. Line a plate with kitchen paper. Fry the toasts in batches for 3 minutes per batch, turning occasionally, until golden and crisp, then remove with a slotted spoon and drain well on kitchen paper. Serve hot with a chilli oil or chilli and black vinegar dipping sauce.

- 280g extra-firm tofu
- 6 spring onions, thinly sliced (including green parts)
- 4–5 fat garlic cloves, finely chopped
- 5cm piece of ginger, finely grated
- 1 tsp dried chilli flakes or togarashi
- 1 tbsp light soy sauce
- 2 tsp toasted sesame oil
- 2 tsp cornflour
- 6 thick slices white stale bread
- 75g panko breadcrumbs
- 1 tbsp each black and white sesame seeds
- 2 eggs, lightly beaten
- Rapeseed oil, for deep frying
- Sea salt
- Chilli and Black Vinegar Dipping Sauce (page 225) or chilli oil, to serve

PILI PILI CASSAVA

Cassava, otherwise known as yucca or mogo, is a starchy, delicious tuber that I would encourage you to get to grips with. In the UK, potatoes are the usual go-to carb but across Africa, Latin America and some parts of Asia too, cassava is by far the more popular choice. It may seem intimidating at first glance, with its rough brown skin and alien root-like appearance, but once you have got rid of the tough exterior it can be boiled, roasted or fried just like a potato and is every bit as delicious. I especially like it fried because the fibrous texture means you end up with lots of those crispy bits everyone always fights over.

———————

Peel the cassava roots using a sharp knife, leaving you with only the white part of the root. Cut the roots lengthways into quarters and remove the woody middle, then cut into 4cm cubes. Bring a large pan of salted water to the boil, then add the cassava and boil for about 30 minutes until a knife goes through them easily. Drain well.

Heat a little rapeseed oil in a wok over medium heat and quickly fry the garlic for 3 minutes until golden brown and fragrant. Heat the remaining oil in a deep-fat fryer or in a deep, heavy-based saucepan (no more than half full) to 180°C – if you don't have a thermometer, you will know the oil is ready when a cube of bread added to the pan turns golden in 20 seconds. Line a plate with kitchen paper. Fry the cassava in batches for about 4 minutes, being careful not to overcrowd the pan, turning them occasionally, until golden and very crisp, then remove from the pan and drain on kitchen paper.

Put the fried cassava into a large bowl and season with salt, sprinkle over chilli powder and then add the garlic, red onion and coriander. Squeeze over the lime juice, toss and serve immediately.

- 2 cassava roots (about 1.5kg)
- Rapeseed oil, for deep frying
- 5 garlic cloves, very finely chopped
- ½–1 tsp red chilli powder
- 1 small red onion, very finely chopped
- Small bunch of coriander, very finely chopped
- Juice of 1 lime
- Sea salt

KFC
(KOREAN FRIED CAULIFLOWER)

A double fry in a light bubbly batter that forms a crisp shell followed by a toss in an addictive chilli sauce mixed with numbing Sichuan peppercorns transforms humble cauliflower florets into a compelling snack. The kimchi, apple and pear salsa (page 208) makes an excellent side.

———————

First make the chilli sauce. Whisk everything together in a small saucepan and cook over low-medium heat for 5 minutes till syrupy. Remove from the heat and set aside.

Heat the oil in a deep-fat fryer or in a deep, heavy-based saucepan (no more than half full) to 180°C – if you don't have a thermometer, you will know the oil is ready when a cube of bread added to the pan turns golden in 20 seconds. Line a plate with kitchen paper.

While the oil is heating, make the batter. Whisk together the dry ingredients, fold in the beaten egg white, then mix in the water a little at a time. Dip the cauliflower florets in the batter and deep-fry in batches for 4–5 minutes until golden and crisp. Remove with a slotted spoon, drain on kitchen paper, then fry again for a second time in batches again for a minute or two to get it extra crunchy. Drain again on kitchen paper then toss in chilli sauce. Sprinkle with sesame seeds and spring onions and serve.

· Rapeseed oil, for deep frying
· 1 large cauliflower, cut into large florets
· Toasted white sesame seeds, for sprinkling
· 4 spring onions, thinly sliced on the diagonal (including green parts)

FOR THE CHILLI SAUCE
· 75g gochujang
· 2 tbsp light soy sauce
· 2 tbsp rice vinegar
· 2 tsp light brown sugar
· 1 tbsp honey
· 2 garlic cloves, finely chopped
· 3cm piece of ginger, finely grated
· ½ tsp Sichuan peppercorns and ½ tsp black peppercorns, toasted and coarsely ground

FOR THE BATTER
· 125g plain flour
· 2 tbsp cornflour
· ½ tsp baking powder
· 1 egg white, beaten to soft peaks
· 150ml ice-cold sparkling water

3
BREADS AND PANCAKES

BREAKING
BREAD

I never gave bread much thought until I stopped
eating it. It was the late nineties – I had just crossed
the threshold into my twenties and was living
away from home for the first time. I had both the
pleasure and terror of being free to do as I liked,
and occasionally asserted my autonomy by making
poor choices that came at the expense of my
wellbeing. One of these expressions of freedom
was a vain, fleeting interest in working as a model
– something my conservative parents would never
have allowed while I was living under their roof.

Aged 20 I was waifish – a little underweight even – but on a shoot for an
Indian bridal magazine I overheard the photographer casually comment
that I was 'photographically fat'. I felt humiliated and let down by my
own body. Back at my student digs, I wept. At the time, the Atkins diet
was at the height of popularity so naturally bread became the enemy.
I shunned carbohydrates, missed meals and numbed myself to natural
cues of hunger. I sought to improve and physically alter the body
I perceived to be flawed. Before then, my encounters with baguettes,
chapattis, parathas, pizza and pancakes had been delicious but
ordinary – they were part of the circular daydream of everyday life.

I rejected the bread basket, but there was a dizzying sense that
something was missing. I became listless, unhealthily thin and felt

hollow. It is easy to fetishise bread when it represents forbidden pleasure. The very thing you have an abject fear of eating becomes the object of desire. I would torment myself by visiting bakeries with lightheaded derangement – oh, the tyranny of their sensory pleasures! I ogled displays of craggy loaves, dimpled bagels, the sensual crevices of golden croissants, and abstained. The smell of yeast filled my nose and the warmth of the oven became an ache in my cold, sad heart. Loss and desire ran through every slice.

A few years later, as part of an assignment for my journalism coursework, I was sent to visit a house where refugee women came together to cook. There were fragrant curries bubbling on the stove and maternal stews, but mostly there was plenty of dough – both leavened and unleavened. There was a range of breads that embodied the multi-ethnicism of the bakers; sweet yeasted plaited loaves similar to Sephardic challah, pockmarked pancakes with a distinctive tang that gained in complexity the more you chewed, and a flatbread fried on a cast-iron pan that combined the flakiness of a croissant and the chew of a paratha. The women smiled broadly and offered me a plate piled high with freshly baked goods. One of them told me that in her native tongue the same word is used for bread and life because bread is life, and what is life without bread? With that wisdom she liberated me from my tense coil of carbohydrate anxiety.

Barely any of women spoke the same language but they didn't need to. There was a tacit communication between them that arose from the gesture of baking and breaking bread together. In the precious and fragile everyday moments of kneading, shaping, buttering and slicing there were silent utterances of friendship, refuge, relief and solidarity. I wanted to cry when they gave me something like a saffron scone with a smear of butter on it like sunshine, puddles of gold soaking into its warm tufts. Eating it was like a communion with an old self I had unnecessarily punished and deprived. It is a miracle of basic ingredients – flour, water and salt – that swell generously to offer something more than the sum of their parts. The world is a better place when there is bread in it.

SAFFRON SHEERMAL

Variations of this sweetly fragrant saffron bread can be found in Kashmir, Armenia and Iran. In India it resembles more of a flaky flatbread like a naan and is eaten with fiery curries where its sweetness lends reprieve. This version is more reminiscent of a brioche-like loaf. Its delicate, lightly sweet crumb has as much in common with cake as it does with bread and can be enjoyed with both sweet and savoury food. Try it with the Date and Orange Blossom Butter (see page 229). This bread is also wonderful served alongside dips like hummus as part of a mezze or with soups like dhal.

———

Gently heat the milk in a pan till it is lukewarm – about 38°C. If you don't have a thermometer, you should be able to put a clean finger into the warm milk and hold it there comfortably. Transfer the milk to a bowl, add the saffron to it and then mix it with the egg, ghee and sugar. Next, add the yeast and mix, then add the salt and the flour and knead lightly. Cover with a damp tea towel and let it rest in a warm place for 1 hour.

Dust a clean worktop with a little flour then gently shape your dough into a circle around 23cm wide. Lay it on a lined baking sheet then, using your knuckles, press a 2cm border around the edge so you have an inner circle. You can leave it like this, or you can use your knuckles to depress 4 lines across the inner circle so you have four quarters. Cover with a damp tea towel and leave to rest in a warm place for another 30 minutes.

Preheat the oven to 180°C/Fan 160°C/Gas Mark 4.

Brush the egg yolk over the surface of the central circle and then sprinkle with sesame seeds. Bake for 25 minutes, then remove from the oven and leave to cool slightly and serve.

· 240ml whole milk
· Fat pinch of saffron threads
· 1 large egg
· 100g ghee
· 100g caster sugar
· 1 tbsp dried instant yeast
· ½ tsp salt
· 450g plain flour, plus extra
  for dusting
· 1 egg yolk, beaten, for brushing
· Black and white sesame seeds,
  for sprinkling

WILD GARLIC BUTTER
TEAR-AND-SHARE ROLLS

It's never pizza – the reason I always need to loosen my belt at a pizzeria is garlic bread. I can't resist its pungent butter-soaked tufts. These rolls are made with a butter infused with wild garlic which grows in abundance every spring. I love the subtle flavour of it at the beginning of the season – like garlic without the fangs. If you can't get hold of wild garlic, roast a whole head of garlic, squeeze out the soft garlic from the cloves and mix with finely chopped parsley to add a vernal freshness. For a cheesy twist, sprinkle some grated Parmesan over the surface before baking – either way it's fiendishly good.

Heat the milk in a pan till it is lukewarm – about 38°C. If you don't have a thermometer, you should be able to put a clean finger into the warm milk and hold it there comfortably. Pour the warmed milk into the bowl of a stand mixer fitted with the dough hook attachment. Sprinkle the yeast and half a teaspoon sugar on top of the milk. Give it a light stir with a spoon and allow to stand for 10 minutes or until it goes frothy.

With the stand mixer running on low speed, add the remaining sugar, the egg, butter, salt, garlic powder, and two-thirds of the flour. Beat on low speed for 1 minute, then add the remaining flour. Continue to beat it for a minute until it comes together and you have a soft, slightly sticky dough. It should pull away from the sides of the bowl as it mixes. When it does, it's ready to knead.

Form the dough into a ball and turn it out onto a lightly floured surface. Knead for 3 minutes, then place into a bowl lightly greased with olive oil. Turn the dough over to coat all sides. Cover the bowl with cling film and place it in a warm place for about 2 hours to rise until doubled in size.

While you are waiting for the dough to rise, make the wild garlic butter. Mix together the butter, wild garlic, lemon zest and a good squeeze of juice and some seasoning together and set aside.

· 240ml whole milk
· 7g active dried yeast
· 2 tbsp plus ½ tsp granulated sugar
· 1 large egg, at room temperature
· 45g unsalted butter, melted, then slightly cooled
· 1 tsp salt
· 1 heaped tsp garlic powder
· 385g strong white bread flour, plus extra for dusting
· A drizzle of olive oil

FOR THE WILD GARLIC BUTTER
· 100g butter, melted
· 20g wild garlic, finely chopped
· Zest of 1 lemon and a squeeze of juice
· Sea salt and black pepper

Once the dough has doubled in size, punch it down to release any air bubbles. Remove the dough from the bowl and turn it out onto a lightly floured surface. Punch it down again to release any more air bubbles if needed. Divide the dough into 12 equal pieces. Shape into balls and arrange into a lightly oiled 24cm round cake tin. Brush the rolls generously with wild garlic butter and sprinkle each with sea salt. Keep any leftover butter aside – it's amazing brushed on the rolls after they are baked too. Loosely cover the rolls with cling film and allow to rise for a further 30 minutes until doubled in size and puffy.

Preheat the oven to 180°C/Fan 160°C/Gas Mark 4. Bake the rolls for 12–15 minutes until golden brown. Brush with the remaining butter if desired.

COURGETTE, PRESERVED LEMON *and* FETA LOAF

This is an incredibly simple and flavourful loaf to bake. It requires no heavy-duty kneading or proving. The feta adds a salty creaminess while the preserved lemons lend a gentle brightness to the bread. I love it spread with hummus or topped with mashed avocado as a simple Sunday brunch.

———————

Put the courgettes in a colander, sprinkle and massage with 1 teaspoon of the salt and set aside for 1 hour to drain out the excess liquid from them. Rinse, turn out onto a clean tea towel, and wring out any excess liquid.

Preheat the oven to 180°C/Fan 160°C/Gas Mark 4. Grease a baking sheet with the olive oil.

In a large bowl, mix together the flour, remaining salt and a generous grinding of black pepper, Turkish pepper flakes, preserved lemon rind, oregano, parsley, feta, egg and milk. Mix to form a soft dough, being careful not to overwork it. Shape into a round and place on the greased baking sheet.

Bake for 40–45 minutes, until the loaf is golden and makes a hollow sound when tapped underneath. Cool on a wire rack then serve warm, sliced, with butter or olive oil.

- 300g grated courgettes (about 2)
- 2 tsp sea salt
- Drizzle of olive oil
- 200g self-raising flour
- 1 tsp Turkish pepper flakes (pul biber)
- 2 preserved lemons, rind only, finely chopped
- 1 heaped tbsp finely chopped fresh oregano leaves
- 30g flat-leaf parsley, finely chopped
- 100g feta cheese, well drained and crumbled
- 1 egg, lightly beaten
- 2 tbsp whole milk
- Black pepper

PESTO *and* SUN-DRIED TOMATO BABKA

This beautiful woven loaf stuffed with grassy pesto that tastes like a mouthful of summer barely makes it to the table before everyone tears at it and devours it. If you can bear to wait, it's ideal for picnics.

———

First make the pesto. Crush the basil, garlic and pine nuts in a pestle and mortar to a coarse paste then gradually add the olive oil, mixing as you go. Fold in the Parmesan, lemon zest and juice, season and set aside.

In a bowl, or a stand mixer fitted with the dough hook attachment, combine the flour, sugar, salt and yeast. In a separate bowl, whisk the oil, egg and water. Add the wet mixture to the dry and knead or mix on a low speed until the dough comes together. If it seems dry, add a little more water – you should have a soft but not sticky dough. Turn it out onto a floured surface and knead for 8–10 minutes until smooth and springy or, if using the mixer, knead on medium speed for 8–10 minutes until the dough comes away from the sides of the bowl and is smooth and springy. Roll it into a ball. Grease the mixing bowl with a little oil, then return the dough to the bowl. Cover with a tea towel and set aside in a warm place for 1 hour or until doubled in size.

- 450g strong white bread flour, plus extra for dusting
- 1 tbsp caster sugar
- 1 tsp salt
- 1 × 7g sachet dried yeast
- 50ml extra virgin olive oil, plus extra for drizzling
- 1 egg
- 200ml lukewarm water
- 150g sun-dried tomatoes, thickly sliced
- 2 tbsp milk, to glaze

FOR THE PESTO
- Big bunch of basil leaves
- 1 garlic clove
- 60g pine nuts
- 100ml extra virgin olive oil
- 50g Parmesan, grated, plus extra to serve
- Zest and juice of 1 lemon
- Sea salt and black pepper

Turn the dough out onto a lightly floured surface and knead briefly. Roll out to a rectangle roughly 40 × 25cm. Spread the pesto over the dough, leaving a 1cm border along the edges. Dot over the sun-dried tomatoes then, using the long edge, roll up the dough into a tight sausage, pressing gently to seal the seam. With a sharp floured knife, cut the sausage in half lengthways, then twist the 2 pieces together to form a rope twist, pushing any tomatoes that pop out back into the bread. Carefully transfer the twisted loaf to a greased 2lb loaf tin, tucking the ends underneath. Cover with a damp tea towel and set aside in a warm place to prove for 40 minutes until doubled in size.

Heat the oven to 200°C/Fan 180°C/Gas Mark 6. Brush the top of the loaf with a little milk. Bake for 35–45 minutes and cover with foil halfway if it is getting too brown. Cool in the tin for 10 minutes, then turn out onto a wire rack to cool. Slice to serve.

LEMON *and* CURRY LEAF CRUMPETS
with LIME PICKLE BUTTER

I find a hot crumpet pretty irresistible, especially with a pat of butter melting into its dimples. The inspiration for these curry-leaf ones come from South India where uttapam – a fermented rice and lentil pancake – has a similar lactic tang and porous surface.

———

Heat the milk and butter in a saucepan over low heat until the butter melts, then leave to stand until lukewarm. Combine the sugar and yeast in a small bowl, add 200ml of the milk mixture, stir to dissolve, then stand in a warm place for 5 minutes until foamy.

Combine the flour and salt in a large bowl, make a well in the centre and add the yeast mixture, stirring to incorporate a little flour. Add the remaining milk, stir until smooth and combined, then cover and stand in a warm place for 1 hour until very foamy.

Dissolve the bicarbonate of soda in the warm water, then beat into the batter. Cover and leave in a warm place for 30 minutes until bubbling.

Now make the tempering. Heat the oil in a frying pan over high heat. Add the mustard seeds and as soon as they pop add the asafoetida and curry leaves. When they crackle add the turmeric and lemon zest and fry for 20 seconds. Pour it over the batter and gently mix in.

Butter 10 crumpet rings or biscuit cutters – I use 9cm diameter 2.5cm-deep rings but use what you have (or go freeform – you'll end up with something more like a pancake, but it'll be delicious nonetheless). Heat a frying pan over low-medium heat. Add a little butter, then place some rings in the pan and fill each two-thirds full with batter. Cook for 4–5 minutes until the mixture bubbles, small holes form on the surface and a skin forms on top. Carefully remove the rings, turn the crumpets and cook for another 4–5 minutes until light golden and cooked through. Keep warm while you cook the rest. Serve immediately with lime pickle butter, or serve toasted the following day.

- 450ml whole milk
- 20g butter, plus extra for cooking
- 1 tsp caster sugar
- 1 × 7g sachet dried yeast
- 250g strong white bread flour
- Pinch of salt
- ½ tsp bicarbonate of soda
- 25ml warm water
- Lime Pickle Butter (see page 229)

FOR THE TEMPERING
- 2 tbsp rapeseed oil
- 1 tsp brown mustard seeds
- ¼ tsp asafoetida
- 15–20 fresh curry leaves
- ½ tsp ground turmeric
- Zest of 1 lemon

VEGGIE BREAKFAST BREAD *and* BUTTER PUDDING

This is the most wonderful way of cooking a full veggie breakfast without all the stress of managing timing and juggling several pots and pans. Mushrooms, spinach, sun-dried tomatoes and brioche are submerged in a cheesy savoury custard and then baked to set, crisp-topped perfection. Best of all, it can be prepared well in advance (I tend to prepare it the night before I want to eat it) and just popped in the oven, leaving you to potter about or spend time with friends.

––––––––

Preheat the oven to 180°C/Fan 160°C/Gas Mark 4 and line a large oven tray with baking paper. Grease a 1.8-litre baking dish liberally with butter.

Heat a little oil in a frying pan and add the baby spinach. Cook until wilted then remove from the heat. Let it cool then squeeze out 75 per cent of the excess liquid from it and roughly chop.

- Olive oil
- 500g baby spinach
- 100g unsalted butter, cut into cubes, plus extra for greasing
- 500g chestnut mushrooms, thickly sliced
- 3 garlic cloves, finely chopped
- 2 red onions, thickly sliced
- 2 tbsp picked thyme leaves
- ½ tsp dried chilli flakes
- 1 tsp caster sugar
- 1 brioche loaf (400g)
- 300g crème fraîche
- 2 eggs, plus 2 egg yolks
- 2 tsp Dijon mustard
- 200ml double cream
- Zest and juice of 1 lemon
- 150g grated mature Cheddar or Gruyere cheese
- 100g sun-dried tomatoes, chopped and drained
- Sea salt and black pepper

Add a little bit more oil to the same pan with a knob of butter and, once the butter is foaming, fry the mushrooms over medium-high heat until they are golden. Add the garlic and continue to fry for 2–3 minutes until fragrant and the mushrooms are dark and golden. Remove from the pan and set aside.

Wipe out the pan with kitchen paper and put it back over low heat. Drizzle in a little more olive oil and add a knob of butter, then add the onions, thyme leaves and chilli flakes and fry for 8 minutes or until the onions are soft and yielding. Sprinkle over the sugar and continue to fry for another couple of minutes till they are dark and caramelised. Set aside.

Cut the brioche into thick slices and then cut diagonally into half and spread on the lined oven tray. Bake, turning occasionally, until golden and toasted. Reduce the oven temperature to 150°C/Fan 130°C/Gas Mark 2. Whisk the crème fraîche, eggs, yolks and mustard in a bowl until smooth, then whisk in the double cream, lemon zest and juice and two-thirds of the cheese, season to taste and set aside.

Arrange the toasted bread in the greased baking dish, in overlapping layers, adding the spinach, mushrooms, caramelised onions and sun-dried tomatoes in between the layers. Once complete, pour the egg mixture over and stand to soak for 30 minutes. Top with the remaining cheese and bake for 45 minutes until golden and a skewer inserted into the bake comes out clean. Set aside to cool slightly then serve.

ROOT VEGETABLE *and* CHESTNUT CAKE *with* PRESERVED LEMON GREMOLATA

Roots and tubers such as swedes, parsnips, beets, celeriac and turnips are lamentably undervalued. They may seem unremarkable and are unlikely win any beauty pageants, but for me these subterranean beauties are diamonds in the rough. If you treat them with a little love and care, roots and tubers are rewarding and dependable – full of sweet, deep and surprising flavours that'll see you through a lean winter. They may look like plain Janes, but the way you cook them doesn't have to be dowdy. This savoury cake celebrates them with a bit of a sexy makeover and gives them a moment to shine. If you keep the size of the root slices fairly uniform, they will cook in pretty much the same time, making them ideal to roast together. Roasting them teases out their natural sugars so they will go spectacularly golden brown and caramelise beautifully on top of the cake. The gremolata, which is full of delectable things like preserved lemon and Turkish pepper flakes, should be doled out liberally to bring a little lightness to the earthy roots and cut through the richness of the cheesy cake. Serve with a little salad as a light lunch or a poached or fried egg for breakfast.

———————

- 350g root vegetables of your choice (I used a mixture of swede, carrots, celeriac, turnip, baby beetroot and Jerusalem artichokes)
- 5 baby onions, halved
- 100ml extra virgin olive oil, plus extra for drizzling
- A few picked thyme leaves
- 1 tbsp honey
- 125g plain flour
- 75g fine polenta
- 2 tsp baking powder
- 1 tbsp dried oregano
- Zest of 1 lemon
- 75g unsalted butter, softened, plus extra for greasing
- 2 tbsp Greek yoghurt
- 100g finely grated Parmesan
- 4 large eggs
- 25g cooked chestnuts, halved
- Sea salt and black pepper

FOR THE PRESERVED LEMON GREMOLATA

- Large handful of flat-leaf parsley, finely chopped
- 1 small garlic clove, finely chopped
- 2 preserved lemons, rind only, finely chopped
- ½ tsp Turkish pepper flakes (pul biber)
- 4 tbsp extra virgin olive oil
- Sea salt and black pepper

Preheat the oven to 180°C/Fan 160°C/Gas Mark 4 and grease and line the base and sides of a 25cm loose-bottomed cake tin.

Chop and slice the root vegetables, keeping their size pretty even (about 5mm) so they all cook through in roughly the same time. Put them in a bowl along with the halved onions and drizzle with oil and add the thyme, season with salt and pepper then drizzle over honey. Toss well.

Mix together the dry ingredients and lemon zest in a medium bowl and set aside.

Cream the butter, yoghurt, Parmesan and 100ml oil in a stand mixer fitted with the whisk attachment until pale and very fluffy. Add the

eggs, one at a time, beating after each addition, until smooth. Fold in the dry ingredients with a metal spoon until combined.

Spoon the batter into the lined cake tin and tap on the surface to level it out. Lay the prepared vegetables and chestnuts over the cake batter then bake for 40–45 minutes until the vegetables are caramelised and a small knife inserted into the centre of the cake comes out clean. Remove from the oven and let the cake cool before removing it from the tin.

To make the gremolata, simply mix together all the ingredients. Serve the cake at room temperature with a generous helping of gremolata.

SPINACH *and* MUNG BEAN CHEELAS *with* AVOCADO *and* COCONUT CHUTNEY *and* SPROUTS

I learnt to make these fortifying Indian pancakes from my grandmother who raved about their health-giving properties. They are gluten free, packed with protein and iron, and are easily digestible. They may not be as iconic as better-known dosas but they are far easier to make, with no fermentation required. Get ahead by soaking your mung beans and rice the night before and you'll wake up to a savoury breakfast that will stand out in the sea of mundane pancakes.

———————

Rinse the mung beans and rice well, then cover with double the amount of water and soak for a minimum of 4 hours or overnight.

In a food processor, blend together the spinach, ginger, chilli and coriander with a little water. Once it's smooth, drain and add the drained mung beans and rice together with cumin seeds and ajwain and salt to taste and blend well. Add the cold water and blend till the mixture has the consistency of a crêpe batter.

To cook the pancakes, lightly oil a cast-iron or non-stick frying pan, tawa or crêpe pan and place over low-medium heat. Pour a ladleful of batter in the centre of the pan and, using the flat back of the ladle, circle and spread the batter to give you a thin pancake. Drizzle some oil on the sides and in the centre of the cheela and then cook for 3 minutes on each side till golden and crisp. Repeat with the remaining batter. Serve with avocado and coconut chutney, a fried egg if desired and a handful of sprouts.

- 100g whole mung beans
- 2 tbsp basmati rice
- 200g spinach, roughly chopped
- Thumb of ginger, peeled and grated
- 1 green chilli, finely chopped
- Handful of coriander, finely chopped
- 1 tsp cumin seeds
- ½ tsp ajwain or carom seeds
- 100ml cold water
- Rapeseed oil, for frying
- Sea salt

TO SERVE
- Avocado and Coconut Chutney (see page 225)
- Fried eggs
- Radish sprouts

SAFFRON MALPUAS *with* NO-CHURN PISTACHIO CREAM

80

If a regular pancake is a girl next door, then these malpuas are a Bollywood sex siren. Once fried to custardy perfection, they are decadently dipped in a syrup perfumed with cardamom and saffron. I first discovered them on a trip to Delhi. It was the holy festival of Ramadan – of the infinite hordes crowding the street food stands at least half of them were there for the malpuas. I have greedily gilded the lily with an easy-peasy no-churn 3-ingredient ice cream that adds another layer of opulence. Make these for breakfast for someone you really love.

———

Begin by making the pistachio ice cream – you can of course buy a ready-made one if you want to skip this step. Put the condensed milk in a bowl and beat in the pistachio paste. Lightly whip the double cream until it holds its shape, then fold it into the condensed milk mixture. Pour into a 1-litre tub and freeze for 4–6 hours.

- Ghee, for frying
- Nibbed pistachios, to garnish

FOR THE PISTACHIO ICE CREAM
- 1 × 450g tin condensed milk
- 150g pistachio paste
- 300ml double cream

FOR THE PANCAKE BATTER
- 175g plain flour
- 50g whole milk powder
- 1 tbsp caster sugar
- ½ tsp ground cardamom
- ½ tsp baking powder
- 350ml cold water

FOR THE SAFFRON SYRUP
- 150ml water
- 250g caster sugar
- Fat pinch of saffron threads
- 4 green cardamom pods, bruised
- 1 tbsp lemon juice

To make the batter for the malpuas, mix the plain flour and whole milk powder in a bowl along with the sugar, cardamom and baking powder. Slowly whisk in the water until you have a thick smooth batter with a pouring consistency. Set aside while you make the syrup.

To make the syrup, heat the water and sugar in a large pan until the sugar has dissolved, then add the saffron and bruised cardamom pods, bring to the boil and simmer for 5–7 minutes. Squeeze in the lemon juice and take off the heat but keep warm.

In the meantime, make your malpuas. Heat a little ghee in a large non-stick frying pan over medium heat then pour a small ladleful of batter into the pan to create a small, round pancake. Cook for 2 minutes, lift up the bottom to check it's golden, then flip it and cook on the other side for 2 minutes. Transfer to a plate lined with kitchen paper and continue cooking the remaining malpuas. Once you have used up all the batter, soak each pancake in the saffron syrup for 20 seconds. Serve warm with pistachio ice cream and nibbed pistachios.

SPICY CAULIFLOWER CHEESE PARATHAS

82

When I was growing up in Kenya, we often took trips en famille to the cobalt-blue coast of Mombasa. For days before our departure my mother paced the kitchen to create an extravagant moveable feast. There would be freshly fried banana crisps – light, thin and resoundingly crunchy – samosas carefully filled with something that tasted like love, old-fashioned fairy cakes with aggressively sweet icing and, most importantly for a clan whose ancestors hailed from Punjab – the breadbasket of India – there had to be plenty of dough. My favourite breads were the parathas, stuffed flatbreads filled with all manner of lovely things such as daikon, cauliflower, unripe (green) papaya or potato. They were fried with ghee on a cast-iron pan so they were cracker-like on the outside but tender within.

What I love the most about parathas is their portability. They are perfect for picnics, road trips, or just for when you need something that you can grab and go that delivers big on flavour. Stuffing parathas requires dexterity. Take handfuls of the stuffing and pile into a dome at the centre of your rolled dough. It is important that the dough is pinched and sealed so that the filling is secure, but this untraditional filling with added Cheddar is quite forgiving. In fact, it's quite lovely if the dough does split in places and some cheese oozes out and crisps up while you are frying. Sometimes beauty (and deliciousness) is to be found in the imperfections.

————

FOR THE DOUGH
· 375g chapatti flour, plus extra for dusting
· 3 tbsp ghee or rapeseed oil, plus extra for shaping and frying
· 300–325ml lukewarm water

FOR THE FILLING
· 1 tbsp ghee
· 1 red onion, finely chopped
· 2 tsp cumin seeds
· Thumb of ginger, peeled and finely grated
· 1–2 green chillies, finely chopped
· 500g cauliflower, grated
· 1 tsp ajwain or carom seeds
· Handful of coriander, chopped
· Juice of 1 lime
· ½ tsp ground turmeric
· 200g extra-mature Cheddar, grated
· Sea salt

To make the paratha dough, put the flour in a large mixing bowl and then rub through the ghee. Now knead in the water a little at a time to form a soft, pliable dough – knead well for 5 minutes until smooth. Cover with a clean damp tea towel and rest the dough while you make the filling.

To make the filling, heat the ghee in a frying pan over low heat, add the onion along with the cumin and fry for 10–12 minutes until caramelised. Next, add the ginger and chillies and fry for a minute or two till fragrant. Add the grated cauliflower and sauté for a few minutes till soft. Season, sprinkle in the ajwain, then stir in the coriander, lime juice and turmeric and leave to cool. Once completely cool, stir in the grated cheese.

Divide the dough into approximately 8 balls. Dust the balls with a little extra flour and keep them covered with a clean damp tea towel to prevent them drying out. Before preparing the parathas, grease your palms a little with the oil. Take one ball in the palm of your hands and flatten it to form a disc that is about 12cm wide. Place an eighth of the filling in the centre and bring the edges together and seal the top (this is similar to making a dumpling). Flatten the top with your hands and, using your fingers, flatten to form a disc that is about 18cm wide. While flattening the disc, try to push the filling in the centre towards to the side. Prepare the rest of the parathas similarly.

Heat a non-stick tawa, crêpe or frying pan over medium-high heat. Add a paratha to the pan and cook for 15–30 seconds until it is lightly speckled. Brush the top of the paratha with a little ghee or oil then flip it over and cook the other side while adding more oil or ghee to the top. Once the underside is golden, turn again and cook the first side again till golden brown. Drain on kitchen paper and repeat with the remaining parathas. Serve with yoghurt, achaar and a cup of masala chai for sheer comfort and joy!

BREAD, CHEESE *and* HERB DUMPLINGS *in an* OMANI LIME BROTH

These herbal dumplings are the definitive way to use up stale bread. As they cook in the broth enlivened with dried limes, they become unfathomably fluffy. It's the kind of dish that will warm you down to your shivering bones. Omani limes can be found easily at Middle Eastern shops and – if stored in an airtight container – last forever. They have a wonderful funky and sour flavour and are useful for adding punch to stocks, stews and syrups for drinks with no effort on your part. Simply pierce or bash them and add to whatever you are cooking to give it an added interest or a new lease of life.

FOR THE DUMPLINGS
· 30g butter
· 1 onion, very finely chopped
· ¼ tsp ground cardamom
· 1 large egg, beaten
· 250g stale sourdough bread, torn into small crumbs
· Zest of 1 lemon
· 50g pecorino cheese, grated
· 1 heaped tbsp plain flour
· 3 heaped tbsp chopped chervil (or parsley)
· 3 tbsp chopped dill
· 2 tbsp chopped tarragon
· 1–2 tbsp milk
· Sea salt and black pepper

FOR THE BROTH
· 1 litre vegetable stock
· 1 carrot, thinly sliced
· 3 celery sticks, thickly sliced
· 4 dried Omani limes, soaked in enough boiling hot water to cover them for 30 minutes
· Juice of ½ lemon
· Sea salt and black pepper

TO SERVE
· 1 tbsp finely chopped fresh parsley or chervil
· 1 tbsp finely chopped dill

First make the dumplings. Melt the butter in a frying pan over low-medium heat, add the onion and sauté gently for 10 minutes until soft and translucent. Set aside to cool.

In the meantime, in a large bowl, combine the remaining dumpling ingredients and then the cooled onion and some seasoning. Add the milk to make a soft dough. With wet hands, form into golf ball-sized dumplings and refrigerate while you make the broth.

In a large saucepan, combine the vegetable stock, carrot and celery and bring to the boil. Pierce the dried limes several times with a fork or a sharp knife and add them to the stock along with their soaking water. Reduce the heat and simmer, covered, for 15 minutes. Add the dumplings and simmer uncovered for 12 minutes until light and fluffy. Season to taste and squeeze in the lemon juice. Divide the dumplings among soup bowls, discard the dried limes, ladle the broth over the top, and serve scattered with the finely chopped herbs.

4
SOUPS, DHAL AND KHITCHADI

SOUPER BOWLS

My taste for soups and dhals developed while acclimatising to my new home in England as a child. The damp and frigid weather meant I was a bundle of maladies – stomach-aches, fever, chills and coughs that seemed to go on for months. I was always cold too, and took to wearing a knitted balaclava and mittens indoors, shedding them only at bedtime when I crawled under several voluminous blankets.

My mother, who was busy trying to navigate the challenges of setting up home in a new country, had little time or patience for me, so being poorly came with the silver lining of her undivided attention. She fussed and fretted, touching the cool back of her hand to my forehead, concocting a prescription of kitchen remedies for almost any ailment; fenugreek seeds steeped in water for weak bones, milk shot with golden turmeric for a snotty nose, shards of toothsome caramel speckled with black pepper for a chesty cough and fennel tea for bellyaches. What broke the monotony of those days were the meals she carried in to me on a tray.

In the half dark, a glass of Lucozade threw a neon light first over her face and then mine as she encouraged me to take slow, careful sips. She skillfully peeled and segmented oranges at my bedside, the smell of citrus lifting my sagging spirit. Then there were the steaming spoonfuls of liquid sustenance, sometimes porridges fragranced with mustard seeds and curry leaves, other times lentil soups bolstered with a handful of rice – soothing, dependable and easy to digest.

Occasionally, when her chores were done, she sat with me, folding her tired shalwar-clad legs into her chest, cheering me up with tales of home. As the steam from the soup dispersed, she'd recall the talkative African grey shouting profanities in our veranda and the puny kittens born in the chicken shed. She wondered if the *jamun* trees were bearing the fruit so sweet it seduced armies of ants to perish drunk and happy, stickily clinging to its branches. Reassuring exchanges between mother and daughter on opposite sides of a soup bowl.

Soup may not excite the appetite, but for me, when the world feels like a wilderness, I find safety, memories of my mother and the place I come from contained in a bowl of it – its presence is therapeutic. To some, it's a joyless gruel that's nutritious enough to keep you alive, but devoid of the flavour or texture that makes life worth living, but I strongly disagree. The sheer variety and the combinations of flavours and textures in a soup can be dazzling. If you are making soups with dried lentils and pulses, invest in a pressure cooker – they will cut down your cooking time by half. They are essential for dhals in Indian households, and like my mother, many women acquire their first one as a wedding gift or, in the old days, as part of the dowry!

I especially love gutsy soups like Indian khitchadis and broths from all over Asia that are fortified with rice and lentils or a tangle of noodles that you need a fork or a pair of chopsticks to wrestle – top them with a riot of garnishes for a happy contrast from crispy shallots, matchsticks of ginger and herbs to softly-boiled eggs to enhance the primal satisfaction of the slurp. I am always uplifted by the promise and hope present in an empty soup bowl, because the possibilities are infinite.

COLD CUCUMBER *and* SHEEP'S YOGHURT SOUP *with* WALNUTS *and* SOFT HERBS

Cool, crunchy and refreshing – there is much more to cucumbers beyond green salad and sandwiches. They are the ideal foil for hot weather and spicy food and pair particularly well with anything lactic like yoghurt or buttermilk. This cooling soup is like air conditioning for the body and soul – ideal for savouring in the garden as the weather heats up. It also makes a rather lovely drink served in a tumbler. Caveat: it needs to be made ahead of time so it can go into the refrigerator to get very cold.

————

Melt the butter in a saucepan over medium heat, add the onion and sauté till meltingly soft and translucent but not caramelised. Now add the cumin and allspice, garlic, bay leaf and cucumber and sauté for 8–10 minutes until the cucumber is tender.

Discard the bay leaf, put the contents of the pan in a food processor and blend until smooth, then cool and refrigerate until very cold.

Finally, stir in the yoghurt, season to taste, then pass through a fine sieve and refrigerate until required.

Serve cold with herbs and walnuts.

· 40g butter, chopped
· 1 large onion, thinly sliced
· 1 tsp ground cumin
· ½ tsp ground allspice
· 2 garlic cloves, sliced
· 1 bay leaf
· 4 cucumbers, seeds removed, finely chopped
· 500g sheep's milk yoghurt or natural yoghurt
· Sea salt and black pepper

TO SERVE
· Picked soft herbs such as dill and chervil
· 50g walnuts, roughly crumbled

GREEN GODDESS DHAL *with* PRESERVED LEMON

This lively dhal is made with bright preserved lemons, greens and herbs. My fridge always seems to be full of handfuls of mineral-rich spinach and ends of herbs so it's perfect for putting them to good use. Feel free to use what you have – in the spring I add wild garlic if I can forage any and in winter I may swap the spinach for more robust kale. The sorrel is skippable but I adore the tartness it brings. Either way it tastes like a vibrantly verdant dose of spring – whatever the season.

––––––––––

Heat the ghee in a large saucepan over low-medium heat, add the onion and fry for 10 minutes until sweet and softened. Add the garlic and cook till fragrant then sprinkle in the dried mint. Fry briefly and add the preserved lemon rind. Add the lentils and pour in the water. Bring to the boil then simmer over low heat for about 30 minutes or until the lentils are very soft and mushy.

In the meantime, put the spinach, sorrel (if using) and herbs in a colander and pour over freshly boiled water, then plunge into ice-cold water. Drain and wring out as much water as possible then blend with a little water in a blender until you have a thick smoothie. Pour the green mixture into the cooked dhal, season with salt and pepper and bring back to the boil and serve immediately.

- 1 tbsp ghee
- 1 onion, very finely chopped
- 2 garlic cloves, finely chopped
- 2 tbsp dried mint
- Rind of 2 preserved lemons, finely chopped
- 250g yellow moong dhal, washed and drained
- 1.2 litres water
- 200g spinach
- 100g sorrel – optional
- Handful of mint
- Handful of dill
- Handful of flat-leaf parsley
- Sea salt and black pepper

93

THE BEST EVER DHAL MAKHANI

Dhal makhani is a thick complex dhal from my ancestral state of Punjab in North India. It is made with black lentils, kidney beans, complex spices and plenty of butter, often simmered for hours over coal. It's a dhal Punjabis get very nostalgic about. I don't have the language to describe the taste of a good one, but it is rustic, smoky, comforting – a mouthful of memory and mourning for the homeland.

———

First make the spice mix by toasting all the whole spices in a hot dry pan over medium heat for a few minutes till fragrant, then pulverise along with the crispy shallots in a spice blender till finely ground. Mix through the powdered spices and garlic powder and store in an airtight jar.

Soak the urid dhal and kidney beans in a bowl of water overnight, then rinse well and drain. Put them in a saucepan, cover with three times their volume in cold water and bring to the boil. Skim, then add the cinnamon stick and cardamom pod. Simmer for 45 minutes–1 hour until the beans are soft enough to crush easily against the side of the pan, topping up the water if necessary, because they should always be covered.

Meanwhile, melt the ghee in a large frying pan over medium heat, add the onion and cumin and cook gently over low heat for 15–20 minutes until soft and golden. Stir in the ginger, garlic and chillies, cook for another minute or so, then stir in two heaped teaspoons of the spice mix. Cook for a minute till fragrant and stir in the tomato puree. Cook for a minute then finally add the fenugreek and cook for a further 5 minutes.

When the dhal is ready, drain it over a bowl, retaining the cooking water, then roughly mash so some of the dhal is squashed and some remains whole. Stir all the dhal into the pan with the sauce, then, over low heat, add just enough of the cooking water to bring it to your desired consistency – I like mine quite thick, rather than to soupy.

Season to taste and serve with a scattering of fresh coriander.

· 200g urid dhal, whole and unhulled
· 40g dried kidney beans
· 1 cinnamon stick
· 1 black cardamom pod, bruised
· 4 tbsp ghee
· 1 onion, finely chopped
· 1 heaped tsp cumin seeds
· Thumb of ginger, peeled and grated
· 3 garlic cloves, peeled and crushed
· 1–2 green chillies, finely chopped
· 30g tomato puree
· 1 tbsp dried fenugreek leaves
· Sea salt and black pepper
· Fresh coriander, finely chopped, to serve

FOR THE SPICE MIX
· 2 tbsp coriander seeds
· 1 tsp cloves
· 2 star anise
· 2 blades of mace
· 2 tbsp crispy onions or shallots
· 1 tsp red chilli powder
· 1 tbsp dried mango powder (amchur)
· ½ tbsp dried powdered ginger
· 1 tbsp ground cinnamon
· A good grating of fresh nutmeg
· 1 tsp garlic powder

KEFIR KHITCHADI *with* BROWN RICE *and* LENTILS

Khitchadi is a soothing Indian dish made of rice and lentils. There are several variations found regionally, the most common made with yellow moong dhal and basmati rice. It has the perfect balance of carbs and protein and is an excellent dish to make if you have overindulged or you are feeling under the weather. This one has a Turkish inflection – the kefir adds both tang and richness and can be easily swapped out for yoghurt.

———————

Heat the oil in a saucepan over low-medium heat, add the onion and sauté for 8–10 minutes until soft but not coloured. Stir in the garlic and cook for a few minutes until fragrant. Pour in the water and bring to the boil. Scatter in the brown rice and lentils and cook for 30–45 minutes till the lentils and rice are both soft.

In a bowl, whisk the kefir, egg and flour-and-water mix then add a ladleful of hot liquor from the rice and lentils and whisk to combine. Pour the yoghurt mix into the rice and lentils, reduce the heat and whisk till it comes to a simmer – do not let it boil as it may curdle. Season to taste.

In a separate pan, melt the butter. Once it is foaming, add the dried mint, lemon zest and juice and Turkish pepper flakes. Stir through the dhal and scatter with the fresh herbs to serve.

- 2 tbsp olive oil
- 1 onion, very finely chopped
- 3 fat garlic cloves, crushed
- 1.5 litres water
- 100g brown rice, washed and drained
- 200g green mung lentils, washed and drained
- 500g kefir
- 1 egg, beaten
- 2 tbsp plain flour mixed with 2 tbsp cold water
- 50g butter
- 2 tbsp dried mint
- Zest and juice of 1 lemon
- 2 tsp Turkish pepper flakes (pul biber)
- Sea salt and black pepper
- 2 tbsp each of roughly chopped mint, dill and parsley, to serve

TAMARIND SAMBHAR
with SEMOLINA *and*
COCONUT UPMA DUMPLINGS

- 250g split pigeon pea or toor dhal, rinsed and drained
- 2 litres water
- 1 tsp ground turmeric
- 1 tbsp coconut oil or ghee
- 1 tsp brown mustard seeds
- ¼ tsp asafoetida
- 15–20 fresh curry leaves
- 1 dried Kashmiri chilli, broken in half
- 6 whole black peppercorns
- ½ cinnamon stick, broken up
- 1 tsp cumin seeds
- 1 heaped tbsp sambhar masala (below)
- Thumb of ginger, peeled and finely grated
- 1 tomato, skinned and grated
- 100g tamarind concentrate
- 25g grated jaggery or soft light brown sugar
- 1 long red chilli, thickly sliced
- Sea salt

FOR THE SEMOLINA AND COCONUT UPMA DUMPLINGS
- 175g semolina
- 1 tbsp coconut oil, plus extra for greasing
- Thumb of ginger, peeled and finely grated
- 1 green chilli, very finely chopped
- ½ tsp ground turmeric
- 600ml water
- 25g freshly grated coconut
- ½ tsp sea salt
- Large handful of coriander, very finely chopped

FOR THE SAMBHAR MASALA
- 1 tbsp coconut oil or ghee, for frying
- 4 dried Kashmiri chillies
- 1 tbsp coriander seeds
- 1 tbsp toor dhal, washed and dried
- 1 tsp fenugreek seeds
- 1 tsp whole black peppercorns

Dhals can be rich and creamy or they can be light, brothy and restorative, much like a classic chicken soup. Unlike a polite European broth, however, this South-Indian-inspired sambhar is rapture in a bowl. It's made with nutty split pigeon peas which are boiled until they are tender enough to be mashed. For all pulses and legumes, I would recommend using a pressure cooker to halve the cooking time, but a regular saucepan is fine too. Once cooked, the pigeon peas are animated with whole spices, fragrant fresh curry leaves and a unique spice mix (masala) tempered in hot fat. Tamarind and jaggery add a happy contrast of sweet and sour.

Sambhars are normally served with dosas or idli – a type of steamed rice cake – but I love these upma dumplings made with semolina, coconut and ginger. They are light, fluffy and comforting and especially wonderful when the temperature has taken a nosedive. They can be rolled ahead of time and steamed when you are ready to eat.

———

To make the semolina dumplings, toast the semolina in a hot dry frying pan over medium heat for 7–8 minutes, stirring regularly until it is lightly golden, nutty and toasted. Remove and wipe out the pan. Melt the coconut oil in the pan over medium-high heat and sizzle the ginger and chilli for 2–3 minutes. Once cooked, sprinkle in the turmeric, fry briefly, then pour in the water. Add the coconut and salt and bring to the boil. Sprinkle in the toasted semolina and cook, stirring, for about 5 minutes, making sure there are no lumps. Take off the heat, cover and leave to steam for 5 minutes then stir through the coriander. Turn out the dumpling mixture into a mixing bowl and let it cool slightly but not go cold. Once it is cool enough to handle, knead it gently and then take golf ball-sized portions and roll them between oiled palms till smooth. Set aside. This recipe should make about 20 dumplings.

To make the sambhar, begin by making the masala. Heat the coconut oil or ghee in a small frying pan over low heat and add all

the ingredients. Sauté for 5 minutes then set aside to cool. Once
cool, blend into a coarse powder and store in an airtight container.
This will make about 5 tablespoons of masala. Wipe out the pan
to use later.

In a large saucepan, boil the toor dhal with the water and the
turmeric for 45 minutes till soft (or use a pressure cooker).

Heat the coconut oil in the small frying pan over high heat, then
sprinkle in the mustard seeds. Once they start to pop, add the
asafoetida followed by the curry leaves and dried chilli. Next, add the
peppercorns, cinnamon and cumin as well as the masala powder and
fry briefly till fragrant. Add the ginger and fry briefly for 1 minute,
then add the tomato, tamarind, jaggery and chilli and cook for 10
minutes. Pour this mixture over the cooked lentils and bring back to
the boil. Cook for another 10 minutes then take off the heat. Season
with sea salt to taste.

Steam the semolina dumplings for 10 minutes until they are glossy
and firm and serve with the sambhar poured over.

HOT & SOUR TOMATO SOUP
with THAI BASIL OIL *and*
CRISPY NOODLES

Good tomato soup is right up there with bubble baths, freshly cut flowers and newly washed sheets when it comes to self-care, but it can also be a bit unimaginative. This Thai-inspired one, with its vibrancy of aromatics such as the lemongrass and coriander, an aniseed Thai basil oil and the tingle of the bird's eye chilli is a playful take on the classic. It's anything but dull, plus it is so invigorating that it can clear a sinus with just a sniff!

———————

To make the Thai basil oil, blanch the basil in a saucepan of boiling water for 5 seconds. Drain and refresh in a bowl of iced water, then drain again and squeeze out the excess water. Transfer to a jug with the oil and blend with a stick blender until smooth. Set aside for 10 minutes to infuse, then strain through a fine sieve.

To make the crispy noodles, heat the oil in a deep, heavy-based saucepan (no more than half full) to 180°C – if you don't have a thermometer, you will know the oil is ready when a cube of bread added to the pan turns golden in 20 seconds. Line a plate with kitchen paper. Cut up the noodles with a pair of scissors then deep fry in batches till they puff up and go crisp – this will take seconds. Remove with a slotted spoon and drain well on kitchen paper.

Put the vegetable stock in a saucepan with the water and a pinch of salt and bring to a simmer over medium heat. Add the shallot and tomatoes and simmer for 20–30 minutes until the shallot and tomatoes are tender. Add the lemongrass, garlic, chillies, ginger, turmeric, lime leaves and coriander root, bring to the boil and simmer for 15 minutes, then take off the heat and let it cool down completely.

Blend with a stick blender or food processor then pass through a sieve and discard the solids. Pour back into the pan and add the pineapple juice, soy sauce and sugar and bring back to a simmer. Squeeze in the lime juice to season. Serve with a drizzle of Thai basil oil and a handful of crispy noodles.

· 500ml good-quality vegetable stock
· 700ml water
· 1 shallot, cut into chunks
· 1.25kg good-quality tomatoes, cut into eighths
· 2 lemongrass stalks, roughly chopped (white parts only)
· 3 garlic cloves, bruised
· 2 red bird's eye chillies, chopped
· Knob of ginger, peeled and sliced
· Thumb of fresh turmeric, sliced
· 6–8 lime leaves, torn
· 1 coriander root, roughly chopped
· 50ml pineapple juice
· 50ml light soy sauce
· 1 tbsp palm sugar or light brown sugar
· Lime juice, to taste
· Sea salt

FOR THE THAI BASIL OIL
· A large bunch of Thai basil
· 125ml rapeseed oil

FOR THE CRISPY NOODLES
· Rapeseed oil, for deep frying
· 100g rice noodles

YOGHURT KADHI *with* SQUASH *and* ONION BHAJIS

This silky soup that is thickened with chickpea (gram) flour gets its tartness from sour yoghurt. It is fragrantly spiced and can be served with rice if you don't want to make the bhajis – although I highly recommend that you do. They are a treat even without the soup and bring it body and heft.

· 400g natural yoghurt (preferably left out overnight to sour)
· 50g chickpea (gram) flour
· ½ tsp ground turmeric
· 1.5 litres cold water
· 2 tbsp ghee
· 1 tsp brown mustard seeds
· Pinch of asafoetida
· 15 fresh curry leaves
· 2 dried whole chillies, broken in half
· ½ tsp cumin seeds
· 1 cinnamon stick, broken up
· 2 cloves
· Thumb of ginger, peeled and grated
· 3 garlic cloves, finely chopped
· 1 green chilli, finely chopped
· 1 heaped tbsp grated jaggery or soft brown sugar
· Handful of finely chopped fresh coriander
· Juice of 1 lime
· Sea salt

FOR THE SQUASH AND ONION BHAJIS
· 225g butternut squash, grated
· 75g chickpea (gram) flour
· 25g cornflour
· 2.5cm piece of ginger, peeled and finely grated
· 1 green chilli, finely chopped
· 2 tbsp freshly chopped coriander
· 15 fresh curry leaves
· 1 tsp coriander seeds, lightly crushed
· ½ tsp ground turmeric
· 1 red onion, thinly sliced
· 50ml cold water
· Rapeseed oil, for deep frying
· Sea salt

First prep the squash for the bhajis. Put the squash in a colander, sprinkle with salt, massage it in, then leave aside to allow the salt to draw out excess moisture from the squash.

To start the kadhi, whisk together the yoghurt, chickpea (gram) flour and turmeric in a large bowl until smooth then add the cold water.

Heat the ghee in a large saucepan over high heat and, once hot, sprinkle in the mustard seeds. As soon as they start to pop, add the asafoetida, curry leaves and dried chillies. Once they crackle, add the cumin seeds, cinnamon and cloves. Turn down the heat, sauté briefly till fragrant then add the ginger, garlic and fresh chilli and sauté for 3–4 minutes till golden. Pour in the yoghurt mix, add the sugar and season with salt. Cook over medium heat, stirring constantly, until it comes to the boil then turn down the heat to low and simmer gently for 15–20 minutes. In the meantime, make the squash and onion bhajis.

Place the salted squash on a clean tea towel, then wring it to squeeze out as much water as possible. Put the chickpea (gram) flour and cornflour in a large bowl and add the ginger, green chilli, fresh coriander, curry leaves, coriander seeds and turmeric. Add the grated squash and onion, season with sea salt and stir in the cold water until you have a thick batter.

To fry, heat the oil in a deep, heavy-based saucepan (no more than half full) to 180°C – if you don't have a thermometer, you will know the oil is ready when a cube of bread added to the pan turns golden in 20 seconds. Line a plate with kitchen paper. Drop heaped tablespoons of the batter into the hot oil and fry for 3–4 minutes until crisp and golden brown. Remove with a slotted spoon and drain on kitchen paper.

Add the chopped coriander and lime juice to the kadhi. Ladle into bowls and serve topped with the squash and onion bhajis.

↓

SWEETCORN *and* COCONUT SHORBA *with* POPCORN *and* CASHEW CLUSTERS

You can make this soup using fresh or frozen sweetcorn, but I especially like to make it at the end of summer before fresh corn on the cob becomes a distant memory. Straining the soup through a sieve may seem like a hassle, but it takes no time at all and is worth it for the velvety, creamy finish. The playful nuggets of popcorn and cashew clusters bring some welcome texture. Store the leftover popcorn clusters in an airtight container – they'll be good for up to two weeks, although they never seem to last that long in my house.

————

· 1½ tbsp rapeseed oil
· 1 tsp cumin seeds
· 2 star anise
· 1 small onion, finely chopped
· ¼ tsp ground cloves
· Thumb of ginger, peeled and finely grated
· 2 garlic cloves, finely chopped
· 1 long red chilli, finely chopped
· 500g sweetcorn kernels, frozen or taken from about 4 cobs
· 1 litre good-quality vegetable stock
· 200ml coconut milk
· Caster sugar, to taste
· Sea salt and black pepper

FOR THE POPCORN AND CASHEW CLUSTERS

· 105g coconut oil
· 50g popcorn kernels
· 75g cashews, toasted and roughly chopped
· ½ tsp roughly crushed fennel seeds
· ½ tsp dried chilli flakes
· ½ tsp sea salt
· 125g honey
· Pinch of bicarbonate of soda

First make the popcorn and cashew clusters. Preheat the oven to 100°C/Fan 90°C/Gas Mark 1. Line a baking sheet with parchment paper. Heat 25g of the coconut oil in a large pot over medium heat and, once it is hot, scatter in the popcorn kernels. Cover with a tight-fitting lid and cook, shaking occasionally, until all the corn has popped. Take off the heat, add the cashews and sprinkle with the fennel, chilli flakes and salt.

Put the remaining coconut oil and the honey in a saucepan and bring to the boil, then simmer for 5 minutes. Add the bicarbonate of soda and stir quickly – it will foam up. Pour the mixture over the popcorn and toss to coat as evenly as possible.

Spread the popcorn mixture out over the lined baking sheet and bake in the oven for 45 minutes, tossing halfway through to ensure it bakes evenly. Take out of the oven and use a spoon to push the mixture into clumps and leave to cool.

To make the shorba, heat the oil in a large saucepan over medium heat, add the cumin seeds and star anise and fry for a minute or so till fragrant, then add the onion and sauté over low-medium heat for 8 minutes till soft and translucent. Sprinkle in the ground cloves and fry briefly then add the ginger, garlic and chilli and fry for about 2 minutes till soft. Add the corn kernels and stir-fry briefly, then add the vegetable stock. Season with salt and pepper, bring to the boil, then turn down the heat to low and cook at a gentle simmer for

15 minutes. Remove and discard the star anise and blend the soup with a hand blender or in a liquidiser till smooth, then strain through a fine sieve into a heatproof bowl. Pour the soup back into the saucepan, stir in the coconut milk and bring to the boil. Season with salt and sugar to taste and serve in bowls topped with the popcorn and cashew clusters.

CAULIFLOWER SOUP *with* CURRIED BROWN BUTTER *and* GRUYERE CROUTONS

This soup turns a short list of accessible ingredients into a sublimely tasty soup. Infusing butter with curry powder is a trick to keep up your sleeve: it is delicious drizzled on potatoes before roasting or used to make a terrific hollandaise.

————

Preheat the oven to 200°C/Fan 180°C/Gas Mark 6.

Cut and trim the cauliflower into small florets. Cube the core and stems. Place half the florets onto a baking tray and season with salt and pepper and drizzle with olive oil. Roast for 20–25 minutes until golden and caramelised then set aside.

To make the curried brown butter, melt the butter in a saucepan over high heat. When it starts to brown, stir in the curry powder. Set aside for 20 minutes then pour through muslin and discard the solids.

Meanwhile, mix together the Gruyere, bread and olive oil in a bowl, pour over half the curry-infused butter and mix. Season, toss and spread on a baking tray lined with baking paper and set aside.

Melt the knob of butter with a drizzle of oil in a saucepan over low-medium heat. Add the onion, thyme, cumin and ajwain and sauté for 8 minutes until the onion is soft but not coloured. Add the garlic and lemon zest and fry for 30 seconds till fragrant then add the raw cauliflower, trimmings, potato and stock. Bring to the boil then reduce the heat and simmer for 20–25 minutes until the potato and cauliflower are soft. Using a food processor or a stick blender, blitz till smooth and keep over low heat while you bake the croutons.

Reduce the oven temperature to 180°C/Fan 160°C/Gas Mark 4 and bake the croutons for 5–8 minutes, tossing halfway through till they are crisp and golden brown.

Divide the soup among bowls, scatter over the coriander, cauliflower and croutons and drizzle with the remaining brown butter.

- 1 large cauliflower
- Olive oil, for drizzling
- Knob of butter
- 1 onion, finely chopped
- A few sprigs of thyme, leaves picked
- 1 tsp cumin seeds
- ½ tsp ajwain or carom seeds
- 3 garlic cloves, thinly sliced
- Zest of 1 lemon
- 2 floury potatoes, peeled and cubed
- 1.5 litres good-quality vegetable stock
- Sea salt and black pepper
- 2 tbsp finely chopped coriander, to serve

FOR THE CURRIED BROWN BUTTER AND GRUYERE CROUTONS
- 80g butter
- 2 tsp curry powder
- 3 tbsp grated Gruyere cheese
- 100g day-old sourdough bread, coarsely torn
- 30ml olive oil

CACIO E PEPE CHICKPEA, ORZO *and* KALE SOUP

Cacio e pepe is a traditional Italian pasta dish made with pecorino or Parmesan, black pepper and a little pasta cooking water that we've all fallen hard for. I've seen its flavour profile adapted to so many dishes from gougères to pizza, and here I have borrowed its flavour for this stunning soup that is like a hearty, cheesy pasta e fagioli.

———————

Heat the oil in a pan over low-medium heat and gently fry the onion for 8–10 minutes until softened but not coloured. Add the garlic and lemon zest and fry for 2 minutes till fragrant. Pour in the stock, cover and bring to the boil, then add the kale and chickpeas and simmer for 5 minutes. Next add the orzo and then beat in the cheese and butter and season with salt and plenty of black pepper. Serve at once with a little extra grated cheese.

· 1 tbsp olive oil
· 1 onion, finely chopped
· 2 garlic cloves, finely chopped
· Zest of 1 lemon
· 1.5 litres good-quality vegetable stock
· 200g curly kale, roughly chopped
· 2 × 400g tins chickpeas, drained and rinsed
· 200g orzo, cooked and drained according to packet instructions
· 150g pecorino or Parmesan cheese, finely grated, plus extra to serve
· 100g cold unsalted butter, cubed
· Sea salt and plenty of black pepper

5
RICE AND GRAINS

THE RICE EATERS

'Remember, don't ask for anything to eat at their house,' my mother warned, 'and even if aunty offers – say "no thank you". I don't want her to think you don't get fed at home.' My mother watched me cross the road to go and play with our neighbour's children – her lips twisted into an anxious pink bow.

Her own mother had died when she was just two, and although her father remarried (and went onto have 6 bouncing baby boys) her upbringing had been devoid of maternal tenderness. When she was 16, my grandfather arranged a marriage and she found herself married to my father and living amidst a chaotic, extended family.

Mum had been primed to be an efficient mother and carer. She had raised her baby brothers, and now she had a new family to tend to. Her entire sense of purpose came from being a home-maker – from keeping our house as neat as a pin, from stitching and mending, laundering and ironing, embroidering and knitting and cooking impressive banquets for a hungry brood that never seemed to stop growing. As a result, she resented anything that threatened to usurp what she saw as her role as the chief cook. She was jealous and possessive of our appetites and begrudged us anything but her own home cooking. Even an innocent roadside snack of roasted corn on the cob seasoned with chilli and lime, nibbled on the way home from school, would send her into an almighty strop. Anything a restaurant, street-food vendor or another housewife could do, she could do better – we knew it, she knew it and she knew we knew it too.

We were a clan whose ancestors hailed from Punjab – the breadbasket of India – so there was always plenty of bread with every meal. Mum was an expert at rolling dough – at making accordion pleats with wholewheat pastry brushed with ghee to make the flakiest parathas, at lifting puffs of chapatti directly off scorching flames with seasoned, naked fingers and at showing us her strange, mute love by wrapping us up in blankets of pillowy naan or deep-fried bhaturas. We were spoilt and well fed, but we still had the animal desire and sharp hunger for the foods of other kitchens.

We hankered after monastic plates of starchy *ugali* – a sort of dense porridge made of ground white maize that our house helpers ate every day, or the rice dishes that our formidable neighbour Mrs Sen churned out of her tiled kitchen. We were lured to her house by the fluffy pilaus cooked in fragrant saffron broth and spicy biryanis studded with whole spices, but my favourite of all were the simple, steaming balls of alabaster rice mixed with sweet dhal she rolled between her thumb and fingers and popped into her children's hungry mouths – no spoon required. I once tried to eat with my hands at home much to my mother's astonishment. She threatened to abandon me at the doorstep of the 'rice eaters' as she loftily called the Sens.

Not one to concede to rivals, rice suddenly became abundant on our dining table and even my father, the staunchest of wheat eaters didn't grumble. There is still a place for grains even where there is bread. Nothing else is able to soak up the flavours around it without falling apart, all while still holding its own, like rice, couscous, quinoa or the multitude of other grains. They are the sinkhole for capturing the essence of everything from curries, dressings or cooking juices. Fresh and filling, they get along with anything and absorb and pull whatever accompanies them into every bite. They are the threads that stitch together everything – that lead you to the very core of a dish. Unsurprisingly, whatever grain my mother turned her hand to was perfect – a fine filigree of separate, fragrant and uniformly swollen morsels. When she wasn't looking, we scooped up orbs of rice into our mouths with our fingers – it always tastes better this way.

CHARRED MARINATED WATERMELON *and* BROWN RICE POKE BOWL *with* PICKLED CARROTS

118

Poke, a dish traditionally made with fresh raw fish and toppings like onions and seaweed, has been popular in Hawaii for decades. More recently, it has become beloved globally as a fast lunch option served on a bed of rice. This is a unique vegan spin on it. Marinating and grilling the watermelon gives it a pleasantly smoky depth of flavour.

———

Place the watermelon in a large dish. Mix all the ingredients for the marinade and pour it all over the watermelon, making sure it is evenly distributed. Cover and chill for at least 4 hours or overnight.

For the pickled carrots, combine all the ingredients in a bowl, season to taste and stand at room temperature to pickle for 1 hour.

Place the rice in a saucepan along with the water and sea salt, bring to a simmer, then reduce the heat to low, cover with a tight-fitting lid and cook without uncovering for 40 minutes. Remove from heat and stand covered for 10 minutes, then uncover and fluff up the rice with a fork.

Heat a griddle pan over medium heat. Remove the watermelon from the marinade and grill for a couple of minutes till caramelised on both sides.

Divide the warm rice among bowls and top with the grilled watermelon, avocado, pickled carrot, and pickling liquid to taste. Scatter with crisp-fried shallots, radishes, cress, sesame seeds and nori and season with togarashi.

- 1 baby watermelon, peeled and cut into triangular wedges 400g brown rice
- 750ml water
- 1 tsp sea salt
- 2 avocados, sliced
- Handful of crisp-fried shallots
- 15 radishes, sliced on a mandoline
- Handful of Asian cress
- Handful of toasted sesame seeds
- 2 sheets of nori, torn
- Togarashi, to season

FOR THE WATERMELON MARINADE
- 2 tbsp tamari
- 2 tbsp mirin
- 1 tsp toasted sesame oil
- 3 tbsp rice vinegar

FOR THE PICKLED CARROTS
- 2 carrots, cut into julienne or spiralised
- 2 tbsp rice vinegar
- 2 tbsp mirin
- 2 tbsp toasted sesame oil
- 1 tbsp finely grated ginger

BEIRUTI JEWELLED NOODLE RICE
with TAHINI SAUCE

You may not find rubies and sapphires hidden among the grains here, but this dish is golden with saffron, rich with ghee and opulent with nuggets of nuts and gem-coloured dried fruits. It makes a terrific centrepiece for any celebratory table and is wonderful with just a spoon or two of yoghurt, tahini sauce or as an accompaniment to a main course.

———

Make the tahini sauce simply by mixing together all the ingredients in a bowl.

To make the rice, heat the ghee in a large saucepan over low-medium heat. Add the vermicelli and fry for 4–5 minutes till it is golden brown. Now add the garlic, spices, pine nuts and almonds and cook again for 2 minutes till the pine nuts are golden. Add the drained rice, season with salt and coat well in the ghee and spices. Toss the rice around lightly till it is toasty and hot then pour in the boiling water and add the barberries. Cover, reduce the heat and simmer for 8–10 minutes or until the rice is cooked through and the water has been absorbed. Fluff up the rice with a fork, pile onto a platter and serve with tahini sauce.

· 1 tbsp ghee
· 125g wheat vermicelli, broken into 2cm lengths
· 3 garlic cloves, thinly sliced
· Large pinch of saffron threads
· 1 cinnamon stick
· 4 green cardamom pods, bruised
· 50g pine nuts
· 50g flaked almonds
· 250g basmati rice, washed till the water runs clear and drained
· 500ml boiling water
· 30g barberries, dried cranberries or currants
· Sea salt

FOR THE TAHINI SAUCE
· 100g thick Greek yoghurt
· 30g good-quality tahini
· Zest and juice of 1 large lemon
· 1 small garlic clove, finely grated

PEANUT *and* GOLDEN RAISIN POHA

Poha is an unpretentious street food in Mumbai often eaten for breakfast or as an afternoon snack. It is made with beaten, flattened rice that is incredibly easy to cook and handy to have in your pantry. You can find it in Indian supermarkets and health-food stores. It comes in various thicknesses, but I recommend buying the medium poha. Simply rinse the rice flakes and then stir-fry with onions, spices and curry leaves. I especially love the crunch of the peanuts and the sweetness of the raisins, and like mine seasoned with plenty of lime juice. Although not traditional because it is a dish in itself, poha is also a great accompaniment to dhal or other Indian curries.

––––––––––

Begin by cooking the potato in plenty of boiling salted water until tender. Drain and set aside.

Put the poha in a sieve and rinse briefly – just enough to make sure all the poha is damp but not sopping wet. Set aside.

Heat the oil in a large frying pan over high heat. Once it is hot, sprinkle in the mustard seeds. As soon as they start to pop and sputter, add the asafoetida and curry leaves and fry briefly. Next, add the cumin seeds, onion and peanuts and stir-fry for 7–8 minutes till the onion is softened and the peanuts are golden. Stir in the chilli, ginger and turmeric and cook for 2 minutes till fragrant then add the potato and poha and mix well. Season with salt and sugar, add the raisins and pour over 100ml cold water and cover. Cook over low heat for 5 minutes then pour in the lime juice and scatter over the coriander. Serve topped with the crisp noodles and grated coconut.

· 1 large Desiree potato, peeled and cut into 1cm cubes
· 400g medium poha
· 2 tbsp rapeseed oil
· 1 tsp brown mustard seeds
· Pinch of asafoetida
· 15 fresh curry leaves
· 1 tsp cumin seeds
· 1 red onion, thinly sliced
· 30g red-skinned peanuts
· 1 green chilli, thinly sliced
· Thumb of ginger, peeled and grated
· ½ tsp ground turmeric
· 1 tsp caster sugar
· 30g golden raisins
· 100ml cold water
· Juice of 1 lime
· Handful of finely chopped coriander
· Sea salt

TO SERVE
· Generous handful of crisp noodles (sev)
· Handful of fresh or frozen grated coconut, defrosted

122

INDONESIAN RICE PORRIDGE *with* TURMERIC BROTH

I came across Bubur Ayam, a fragrant chicken congee, when I was travelling in Indonesia. My husband Nadeem caught a travel bug and it was recommended by the chef at the hotel for its soothing and miraculous healing properties. Needless to say, after a few bowls of this, Nadeem was immediately less grouchy and I have been cooking versions of this ever since. I have made this vegetarian version with a powerful turmeric broth that allows you to customise it to thick porridge or thin and soupy depending on how you are feeling. Either way, it is health in a bowl.

———————

First make the turmeric broth. Put all the ingredients for the paste in a food processor with a little water and blend to paste. Heat the oil for the broth in a large saucepan over low heat, add the turmeric paste and fry for about 8 minutes until it changes colour and becomes fragrant. Pour in the vegetable stock and let come to the boil, then reduce the heat to low and simmer while you make the rice porridge.

Bring 1 litre of salted water to the boil in a large saucepan and blanch the green beans, then drain and refresh in ice-cold water. Use the same pan to make the porridge. Wash the rice in cold water and drain. Bring the vegetable stock to the boil, add the star anise, bay leaf and ginger, then drop in the rice. Reduce the heat to low, cover and simmer gently for 20–25 minutes until the rice has broken down. Season to taste.

Ladle the rice porridge into serving bowls, top with the green beans, crispy shallots, chilli, spring onions and coriander leaves. Pour over the turmeric broth and serve at once. If serving at the table, I like to pour the broth into a Thermos flask or teapot so everyone can help themselves.

FOR THE TURMERIC BROTH PASTE
· 2 small banana shallots, roughly chopped
· 5 garlic cloves
· 1 tsp coriander seeds, toasted and ground to a coarse powder
· 1 tbsp macadamia nuts
· 2 lemongrass stalks, roughly chopped
· 6 lime leaves, shredded
· 2.5cm piece of ginger, peeled and roughly chopped
· 5cm piece of fresh turmeric, peeled and roughly chopped
· A good grinding of fresh black peppercorns
· 2 tbsp rapeseed oil

FOR THE TURMERIC BROTH
· 2 tbsp rapeseed oil
· 1 litre good-quality vegetable stock
· Sea salt

FOR THE RICE PORRIDGE
· 200g jasmine rice
· 1 litre good-quality vegetable stock
· 1 star anise
· 1 bay leaf
· 2cm piece of ginger, cut into rough slices
· Sea salt

TO SERVE
· 250g green beans
· Handful of crispy shallots
· 1 red chilli, sliced on the diagonal
· 4 spring onions, sliced
· Picked coriander leaves

ROASTED CARROT *and* HAZELNUT SALAD *with* FREEKEH, DATES *and* ORANGE BLOSSOM WATER

There's a lot to love about freekeh – a green wheat product that is popular throughout the Middle East. It has a pleasing chew and a smoky flavour that comes from the harvesting process. The berries are picked while they are still young and green, and then carefully roasted in the husk over open fires before being beaten to remove the chaff. I love it for salads like this one where it lets the caramelised carrots shine, or added to soups for heft.

———

Preheat the oven to 200°C/Fan 180°C/Gas Mark 6.

Scrape the carrots and cut in half lengthways. Lay in a roasting tray. Melt the spiced honey and saffron butter in a saucepan over low heat and add the preserved lemon. Stir, then pour over the carrots. Cover the tray tightly with foil and cook for 20 minutes, then remove the foil and cook for a further 10–15 minutes, till the carrots are tender and caramelised. Sprinkle over the orange blossom water, cover with foil and let them steam in the perfume.

In the meantime, dry-toast the freekeh in a frying pan over medium heat for 3–4 minutes till toasty. Pour the water into a saucepan, add the salt and bring to the boil over medium-high heat. Sprinkle in the toasted freekeh, stir, bring back to the boil and cover with a lid. Reduce the heat to low and cook for 15 minutes, or according to packet instructions, until the freekeh is tender and the water has evaporated, then drain and transfer to a serving platter. Mix together the oil, lemon juice and some seasoning, pour over the freekeh and toss. Once cool, add the dates and toss with half the hazelnuts and herbs then top with the roasted carrots. Finish by scattering over the remaining herbs and hazelnuts.

FOR THE CARROTS
· 300g small yellow carrots
· 300g small orange carrots
· 100g Spiced Honey and Saffron Butter (page 229)
· 1 preserved lemon, rind only, very finely chopped
· A few drops of orange blossom water

FOR THE FREEKEH
· 200g freekeh
· 400ml water
· 1 tsp salt
· 60ml extra virgin olive oil
· Juice of ½ lemon
· 60g dates, sliced (I can't resist the ones by Zaytoun)
· 50g toasted hazelnuts, coarsely chopped
· Handful of finely chopped flat-leaf parsley or chervil
· Sea salt and black pepper

HOT & SOUR
SWEETCORN RISOTTO *with*
LIME LEAF BUTTER

Once you master a basic risotto it is open to many interpretations and this one is perhaps my favourite. It brings an element of surprise and delight to a dish that is often the 'safe' vegetarian option. The star of the show here is the punchy Thai-inspired hot and sour broth – it absorbs and adds flavour to each swell of rice while the lime leaf butter brings a wonderfully acidic richness that still makes it feel light.

———————

Cut the kernels off the cobs and set aside. Chop the cobs into thirds for the stock. I like to make the stock in advance (at least 4 hours, or overnight) to allow the flavours to infuse. To make it, put the stock ingredients and cobs in a deep pan and bring to the boil. Reduce the heat and simmer for 30 minutes then set aside and leave to infuse.

To make the lime leaf butter, fry the lime leaves in a little oil for 20 seconds till crisp. Drain on kitchen paper then blend to a powder in a food processor and mix with the softened butter and lime juice and zest. Refrigerate until needed.

Strain the stock into a saucepan and discard the solids. Bring to the boil then turn the heat down to low and start making the risotto.

In a food processor, blitz a quarter of the corn kernels with 1 tablespoon of the stock until smooth and creamy, then set aside. Heat the oil and butter in a large saucepan or casserole dish over low heat, add the shallots and cook for 6–8 minutes until soft but not browned. Add the garlic and chillies and fry till fragrant, then turn up the heat, add the rice and stir for a couple of minutes. Add the wine and let it evaporate. Now turn the heat down to medium-low and start adding stock a ladleful at a time, allowing it to absorb as you stir. When half the stock has been added, stir in the whole kernels, then continue adding stock until the rice is cooked but still has a little bite to it, and the corn is tender. This should take about 25 minutes. Stir in the pureed corn and cook for 2 minutes then take off the heat and beat in the lime leaf butter. Serve topped with kale crisps, crispy shallots and more sliced chilli if desired.

FOR THE RISOTTO
- 4 corn on the cob
- 1 tbsp rapeseed oil
- Knob of butter
- 2 banana shallots, finely chopped
- 2 garlic cloves, finely chopped
- 2 green chillies, very finely chopped
- 200g carnaroli risotto rice
- 250ml dry white wine
  Sea salt and black pepper

FOR THE STOCK
- 6 garlic cloves, bruised
- 3 lemongrass sticks, roughly chopped
- Thumb of root ginger, thickly sliced
- 2.5cm piece of turmeric, thickly sliced
- 2 shallots, quartered
- 8 lime leaves, torn
- 3 red bird's eye chillies, slit
- 1 tomato, quartered
- 1 coriander root
- 1.2 litres water

FOR THE LIME LEAF BUTTER
- 10 lime leaves
- Rapeseed oil, for frying
- 50g unsalted butter, softened
  Zest and juice of 1 lime

TO GARNISH
- Handful of kale crisps
- 2 tbsp crisp-fried shallots
- 1 red chilli, sliced – optional

FERMENTED RICE, LENTIL, BEETROOT *and* COCONUT HAANDVO

Haandvo is a delicious savoury 'cake' with the most irresistible crispy surface and edges dotted with sesame seeds and spices that are similar to 'tahdig', the much-loved crust in Persian rice. While it is cake-like it has none of the traditional eggs and flour – instead it is made from a batter of fermented rice and lentils. Start your batter the day before baking to give it plenty of time to ferment and go bubbly. I have used beetroot here, but you can use grated courgettes, butternut squash, sweetcorn, or the more traditional bottle gourd. Whatever you use, I can guarantee you'll be fighting over the crispy bits.

· 250g basmati rice
· 75g channa dhal or yellow split peas
· 75g toor dhal
· 1 tbsp semolina
· 200g natural yoghurt
· ¼ tsp fenugreek seeds
· Neutral oil, for greasing
· 500g grated purple beetroot (about 2)
· 100g fresh or frozen grated coconut, defrosted
· 2 green chillies, very finely chopped
· Thumb of ginger, peeled and grated
· Handful of finely chopped coriander
· 2 heaped tbsp caster sugar
· 1 tsp bicarbonate of soda
· 1 tsp baking powder
· Juice of ½ lemon
· Sea salt

FOR THE TEMPERING
· 6 tbsp rapeseed oil
· 2 tsp brown mustard seeds
· ¼ tsp asafoetida
· 15 fresh curry leaves
· 2 dried Kashmiri chillies, broken up
· 1 cinnamon stick, broken up
· 2 heaped tsp white sesame seeds

Place the rice and lentils in a large sieve and wash with plenty of cold water until the water runs clear. Drain and place in a large bowl and soak in 1 litre of cold water for 4 hours or overnight.

Rinse again, then drain the rice and lentils and grind in a blender with about 100ml cold water until you have a creamy, smooth batter. Pour the batter back into a large bowl and beat in the semolina, yoghurt and fenugreek seeds. Cover with cling film and leave to ferment at room temperature overnight – this will take 6–12 hours. You'll be able to tell it's ready when you see a few bubbles appear on the surface.

Preheat the oven to 180°C/Fan 160°C/Gas Mark 4. Grease a 20cm square cake tin with oil. Stir the beetroot, coconut, chillies, ginger, coriander, sugar and salt to taste into the batter, mix well and set aside while you make the tempering.

Heat the oil for the tempering in a frying pan over high heat. As soon as it is hot, sprinkle in the mustard seeds. Once they start to pop and sputter, add the asafoetida, curry leaves, chillies and cinnamon. Fry briefly for 30 seconds then take off the heat. Discard the cinnamon. Pour half the tempering oil (avoiding the curry leaves and Kashmiri chillies) into the batter and mix well. Add the sesame

seeds to the remaining oil while it's still hot and set aside. Now add the bicarbonate of soda, baking powder and the lemon juice to the batter. It will fizz immediately. Mix vigorously – it will almost double in volume. Immediately pour into the greased baking tin and spoon the remaining tempered oil over the surface evenly. Bake for 1 hour 30 minutes until dark golden brown or until a skewer inserted into the centre comes out clean. Cool in the tin for 1 hour then turn out, slice into 12 squares and serve.

FRAGRANT BULGHUR PILAF *with* QUINCE *and* GOLDEN ALMONDS

When I think of pilafs, I generally think of gently spiced rice cooked with meat or fish. This version is influenced by Turkey where bulghur is commonly used and, rather than meat, I have used the most fragrant fruit of the autumn – quince. It's unusual, delicious and decadent all at once.

————

Peel and halve the quinces, squeeze lemon juice over and rub into the flesh, then steam the quince halves over a saucepan of simmering water for 20 minutes or until just tender. Set aside till cool, then cut into wedges.

Heat 1 tablespoon of the ghee in a casserole dish over low heat, add the onion and fry for 15 minutes until caramelised. Add the almonds and cinnamon and stir for a minute or two till toasted. Remove from the pan and set aside. Now pour the remaining ghee into the dish and add the honey. Let it bubble over high heat until it starts to caramelise. Gently add the quinces and cook for 3–4 minutes till they are caramelised, then remove from the pan and set aside.

Toss the onion and almonds back into the dish. Sprinkle over the ground ginger, coriander and cumin and fry till fragrant and the almonds are golden, then scatter in the bulghur and preserved lemon, season and toast the bulghur grains then pour in the boiling stock. Cover the dish, reduce the heat to low and simmer for 10 minutes or until the bulghur has absorbed the stock. Return the quinces to the pan and cover the bulghur again, leaving it to steam for a further 3–4 minutes. To serve, drizzle over the saffron milk, leaving some of the bulghur stained and some plain, and scatter over the golden sultanas, crispy shallots, parsley and rose petals.

- 2 quinces
- Juice of 1 lemon
- 60g ghee
- 1 onion, thinly sliced into crescents
- 60g flaked almonds
- 1 cinnamon stick, broken up
- 1 tbsp honey
- 1 tsp ground ginger
- 1 tsp ground coriander
- 1 tsp ground cumin
- 250g bulghur wheat, washed and drained
- 1 preserved lemon, rind only, thinly sliced
- 500ml boiling vegetable stock
- Sea salt

TO SERVE
- Large pinch of saffron threads soaked in 60ml warm milk
- Handful of golden sultanas
- Handful of crispy shallots
- Handful of finely chopped flat-leaf parsley
- Handful of dried rose petals

SOFT POLENTA *with* BRAISED FENNEL, OLIVES, CAPERS *and* PANGRATTATO

132

Polenta is a starch that can be served instead of mashed potatoes, rice or pasta. It can be eaten hot with plenty of butter, or spread in a tray, cooled and then cut and fried like chips. This silky Parmesan-rich version is my favourite. I love it with garlic-laden wild mushrooms, sausages or a lentil ragu, but this version with caramelised, braised fennel makes for a great summer dinner party dish.

———

FOR THE PANGRATTATO
· 200g day-old sourdough bread, crusts removed
· 1 garlic clove, finely chopped
· Large handful of parsley, finely chopped
· 2 tbsp olive oil
· Zest of 1 lemon
· 1 tsp Turkish pepper flakes (pul biber)

FOR THE BRAISED FENNEL AND OLIVES
· 3 tbsp olive oil
· 3 medium fennel bulbs, thickly sliced into wedges, fronds reserved
· 1 head of garlic, cloves separated but left unpeeled
· 2 lemons, cut into wedges
· 90g good-quality green olives
· 2 tbsp capers in brine, washed and drained
· 250ml white wine
· Sea salt and black pepper

FOR THE POLENTA
· 1 litre vegetable stock
· 150g fine polenta
· 60g unsalted butter
· 80g finely grated Parmesan cheese
· Extra virgin olive oil, for drizzling
· Sea salt and black pepper

For the pangrattato, preheat the oven to 220°C/Fan 200°C/Gas Mark 7. Tear the bread, put it in a food processor and blend till you have coarse crumbs. Combine with all the other ingredients in a bowl and season to taste. Scatter over an oven tray and bake, shaking occasionally, for 6–8 minutes until golden brown and toasty.

To make the braised fennel, put a large wide casserole dish on your hob. Heat the olive oil in the dish over low-medium heat then lay over the wedges of fennel in one layer and cook for 5 minutes on each side or until coloured and caramelised. Add the garlic, lemons, olives and capers and toss, then pour in the wine and bring to the boil. Cover the dish, turn the heat down to low and simmer for about 25 minutes until the fennel is tender. Mix well and squash the lemon and garlic with the back of your spoon, then pick out and discard the rinds and skins – you don't have to be too precious about this. Mix the fennel well and let it cool to room temperature while you make the polenta.

For the polenta, bring the stock to a simmer in a saucepan over medium heat, then gradually add the polenta, whisking continuously to combine. Reduce the heat to as low as it will go and simmer, whisking occasionally, then more frequently as the mixture thickens, and cook for about 15 minutes. Whisk in the butter and Parmesan cheese and season with salt and pepper.

To serve, spoon the polenta onto plates, top with fennel and all the juices, drizzle over extra virgin olive oil and top with pangrattato and picked, reserved fennel fronds.

6
PASTA AND NOODLES

USE YOUR NOODLE

Asking friends how they are these days seem to have a default answer. 'Busy' they say, 'Super busy!' 'Oh – crazy busy!' 'Back to back!' We are a generation of project jugglers and calendar maximisers. Our busyness is mostly self-imposed. We're ambitious and driven, addicted to noise and anxious about what we might have to examine when we're still. So, we hop about like Duracell bunnies on steroids – scheduling work meetings, doing school runs, tearing about from one social occasion to another, adding a bunch of extracurriculars just for fun. Most nights we walk through the front door thinking, 'What a day!' But there are well-stocked kitchens, hot showers, warm beds – made up if we are lucky – and we are grateful.

On evenings like this, there is a strong temptation to curl up on the couch, in the shape of an elbow macaroni and dial-in a delivery. But I coax myself to cook because the kitchen invites a quiet meditation, an absorption in mindfulness that I crave and need. When I am tired, I want food that gives me, and the ones I am feeding, maximum pleasure with minimum fuss. What that is is subjective – one woman's

instant ramen is another woman's rock bottom – but pasta and
noodles are high on the list for many. They are fast, filling, comforting,
versatile and invite improvisation. They're crowd-pleasers that liberate
us from the tyranny of having to please. A bowl piled up with glossy
enigmatic loops of bucatini is my love language. Best of all they can be
eaten with little commotion – just a fork and an uninterrupted view of
the television.

Pasta and noodles are multifaceted wonder foods and great vehicles
for flavour, yet they seem to be sublimely confident – they have their
own eloquence, an assertive pleasure in their own identity. They are
restrained and don't require too much flourish, but can just as well
handle an anarchy of ingredients with grace. In the weeks after my
father died, linguine slick with butter emulsified with snowflakes of
Parmesan cheese kept me from passing out. I ate forkfuls of it through
convulsions of grief. On other rough days I have been revitalised by
submerging in the soothing comfort of a noodle soup that was like
a bath for the spirit. There are few things that bring joy like their
springy al dente geometry, their primal slurp and satisfying chew.
As you wind their tangle around the tines of your fork, you will feel
yourself unwind.

LASAGNA *of* ROASTED SQUASH, KALE *and* WALNUTS

Lasagna has oodles of appeal. This one has layers of pasta sandwiching roasted squash, ricotta and kale, sage butter, tomato sauce, walnuts and plenty of cheese. I find the repetitive motion of building the layers incredibly calming too. A good one to make on a rainy afternoon. Use fresh pasta sheets for ease.

————

- 800g delica or butternut squash, cut into bite-sized cubes
- 3 red onions, cut into wedges
- 1 tsp fennel seeds
- ½ tsp dried chilli flakes
- 15 sage leaves, plus extra to garnish
- Drizzle of olive oil
- 100g toasted walnuts, roughly chopped
- 250g fresh lasagna sheets
- 100g Parmesan cheese, grated
- 125g buffalo mozzarella
- Sea salt and black pepper

FOR THE TOMATO SAUCE
- Drizzle of olive oil
- 4 garlic cloves, finely chopped
- ½ tsp dried chilli flakes
- 1 tbsp dried oregano
- 2 × 400g tins chopped tomatoes
- 1 tsp caster sugar
- Sea salt

FOR THE KALE AND RICOTTA
- 400g curly kale
- Knob of butter
- 500g ricotta
- 250g mascarpone
- 40g Parmesan cheese, grated
- 4 egg yolks
- Zest of 1 lemon
- A good grating of nutmeg

Preheat the oven to 200°C/Fan 180°C/Gas Mark 6.

Lay the squash and onions in a roasting tin and scatter over the fennel seeds, chilli flakes and sage leaves. Drizzle with oil then roast for 25–30 minutes until tender and caramelised then set aside.

Meanwhile, make the tomato sauce. Heat the oil in a saucepan over low-medium heat, add the garlic and fry for a minute, then add the chilli flakes, oregano and tomatoes. Add the sugar, season, reduce the heat and simmer for 15–20 minutes until thickened.

For the kale and ricotta, blanch the kale in salted boiling water until it has wilted. Drain in a colander then squeeze out any excess water. Roughly chop and mix with the rest of the ingredients and season to taste.

Spread a quarter of the ricotta and kale mix in a 2-litre baking dish, top with half of the roasted squash and onions and crumble over a third of the walnuts. Cover with slightly overlapping lasagne sheets, pour over a third of the tomato sauce. Build another layer with another quarter of the ricotta and kale mix, sprinkle over a little cheese and pour over another third of the tomato sauce. Cover with another layer of lasagne sheets and top with another layer of ricotta and kale, the remaining squash, sage and onions, another third of the walnuts and the remaining tomato sauce. Top with another layer of lasagne sheets and finally spread over the remaining ricotta and kale, scatter over the remaining Parmesan cheese and tear over the mozzarella. Bake for 30 minutes until golden and bubbling. Scatter over the remaining sage leaves and walnuts and bake for another 8 minutes until the sage crisps up. Serve hot and bubbling from the oven.

RIGATONI *with*
30 CLOVES OF GARLIC
and TOMATO SAUCE

This simple pasta sauce is a guaranteed route to happiness. Thirty cloves of garlic might seem like an alarming amount, but when they are cooked slowly in oil and butter, they mellow out, caramelise and lose their fangs. When crushing the garlic, keep it coarse – it's wonderful to find a chunk of a fudgy clove nestled in the hollow of a piece of pasta.

———

Melt the butter along with the oil in a casserole dish over low heat. Add the garlic and let the cloves cook slowly for about 15 minutes, turning them occasionally until they are beautifully soft. Use the back of a fork to roughly crush them. Now add the chilli flakes, oregano and lemon zest. Finely chop the stems of the basil and add those too and infuse over low heat for a further 6–8 minutes.

Pour in the chopped tomatoes plus the water, add the pinch of sugar and season well and bring to the boil. Once bubbling, reduce the heat and simmer for about 30 minutes or until the sauce has thickened to your liking.

Cook the rigatoni in plenty of salted boiling water according to packet instructions. Drain, reserving 50ml of pasta water. Add the drained pasta and pasta water to the sauce as well as the lemon juice and toss. Serve with torn basil leaves and a generous helping of grated Parmesan cheese.

- 100g butter
- 100ml olive oil
- 30 garlic cloves, peeled
- ½ tsp dried chilli flakes
- 1 tbsp dried oregano
- Zest of 1 lemon and juice of ½ lemon
- Handful of fresh basil
- 2 × 400g tins chopped tomatoes
- 400ml water
- Pinch of sugar
- 500g rigatoni
- Sea salt and black pepper
- Freshly grated Parmesan, to serve

LENTIL *and* CHESTNUT DAN DAN NOODLES

Dan dan noodles are the quintessential Sichuanese street food, in which bouncy noodles are dropped into a fragrant, mouth-numbing sauce made with soy, Sichuan peppercorns and usually meat. There are several variations, and this is my vegan version made with the wonderful meaty texture of ready-cooked lentils, umami-packed mushrooms and chestnuts. The sauce has a tantalising numbness from ground Sichuan peppercorns, sharpness from Chinese black vinegar and creaminess from tahini. It's one that will make you flush pleasantly and is ideal for eating when the temperature goes south. Have one bite and you'll want another. Finish up your bowl and you'll be planning your next. This dish is fiercely addictive.

————

In a bowl, mix together the lentils, mushrooms and chestnuts with the mirin, soy sauce and sesame oil and season with white pepper. Mix well and set aside for 30 minutes.

To make the sauce, heat the oil in a wok over medium-high heat, add the ginger and fry for a couple of minutes till fragrant. Next add the lentil mix and stir-fry for 10 minutes till the mushrooms and chestnuts are a little crisp and caramelised. Whisk together the remaining ingredients together in a bowl or jug then pour the mixture over the lentils. Bring to the boil and simmer for 5 minutes.

Divide the warm noodles among bowls, spoon over the sauce and serve immediately scattered with spring onions and sesame seeds.

· 250g ready-cooked brown lentils, drained
· 200g chestnut mushrooms, very finely chopped
· 100g cooked chestnuts, roughly chopped
· 1 tbsp mirin
· 1 tbsp light soy sauce
· 1 tsp toasted sesame oil
· Ground white pepper, to taste
· 400g wheat noodles of your choice, cooked according to packet instructions and drained

FOR THE SAUCE
· 1 tbsp rapeseed oil
· Thumb of ginger, peeled and finely grated
· 30ml light soy sauce
· 30ml dark soy sauce
· 3 tbsp chilli oil
· 1 heaped tsp light brown sugar
· 50ml tahini
· 50ml Chinese black vinegar
· 2 tsp Sichuan peppercorns, toasted and coarsely ground
· 175ml good-quality vegetable stock

TO SERVE
· 3 spring onions, thinly sliced (including green parts)
· Toasted sesame seeds

PASTA FATTEH *with* TAHINI YOGHURT *and* CARAMELISED ONIONS

142

Fatteh is a layered Levantine feasting dish which normally combines layers of meat or pulses, ladles of garlic-spiked yoghurt and toasted Arabic bread but I have used pasta instead for a wonderfully fuss-free summer dinner.

————

To make the tahini sauce, simply mix together all the ingredients in a large bowl and season to taste. Set aside while you cook the onions.

Heat the oil in a frying pan or casserole dish over low-medium heat, add the onions with the cinnamon and bay leaf and fry for 8 minutes until soft and translucent. Scatter in the garlic and fry for 2 minutes till fragrant then add the allspice and continue to fry over low heat until the onions are sticky and caramelised.

Cook the pasta in plenty of salted boiling water according to packet instructions till al dente. Drain, put in the bowl of tahini yoghurt, scatter over the caramelised onions (discard the cinnamon) and mix well. Clean out the pan and return to the heat. Melt the butter in the pan and, once foaming, add the mint and Turkish pepper flakes and cook for 30 seconds. Take off the heat.

Spoon the mint butter over the pasta then scatter over the pine nuts and parsley and serve.

· 2 tbsp olive oil
· 4 medium red onions, thinly sliced
· 1 cinnamon stick
· 1 bay leaf
· 3 garlic cloves, finely chopped
· 1 heaped tsp ground allspice
· 400g pasta shapes (I like to use strozzapretti or cavatelli)
· Sea salt and black pepper

FOR THE TAHINI SAUCE
· 500g Greek yoghurt
· 75g tahini
· 1 garlic clove, finely grated or chopped
· Juice of ½ lemon
· Sea salt

TO TOP
· 40g butter
· 2 tsp dried mint
· 1 tsp Turkish pepper flakes (pul biber) or mild dried chilli flakes
· Handful of toasted pine nuts
· Handful of finely chopped parsley

144

SAFFRON, CAULIFLOWER *and* MACARONI BAKE

Mac 'n' cheese and cauliflower cheese are both ultimate comfort foods and this dish sits right in the middle of the two. The florets of cauliflower and pasta are draped in a velvety béchamel gently spiced with saffron and curry powder, bringing a little interest and frisson to an otherwise mellow dish. Serve with a crisp green salad to offset the richness.

———

Preheat the oven to 180°C/Fan 160°C/Gas Mark 4.

Cook the macaroni in a large saucepan of boiling salted water for about 5 minutes until al dente, adding the cauliflower after 2 minutes. Drain and set aside.

Clean out the pan and melt the ghee over low-medium heat, then add the onions and fry for 8–10 minutes until golden and caramelised. Add the garlic, Madras curry powder and saffron – adding more ghee if needed – and fry again for 2 minutes till the spices are fragrant.

For the béchamel, add the butter to the pan of curried onions and let it melt, then add the flour and stir and cook for 3–4 minutes until sandy. Gradually whisk in the warmed milk a little at a time and stir until it has thickened. This will take 3–4 minutes. Stir in the cheese and coriander, season with sea salt and pepper and tumble in the cauliflower and pasta, stirring well to make sure it is all evenly coated. Turn out into a 25 × 35cm baking dish and scatter with a little more grated cheese.

Mix the breadcrumbs and almonds together with the olive oil and scatter over the surface of the cauliflower and pasta mix. Bake for 25–30 minutes until golden brown and bubbling. Serve at once.

· 300g macaroni or other pasta shape
· 1 small cauliflower (about 650g), cut into florets
· 1 tbsp ghee
· 2 onions, finely chopped
· 4 garlic cloves, finely chopped
· 1 heaped tbsp Madras curry powder
· Fat pinch of saffron threads
· 100g panko breadcrumbs
· 50g flaked almonds
· 1 tbsp olive oil
· Sea salt and black pepper

FOR THE BÉCHAMEL
· 100g butter
· 4 tbsp plain flour
· 500g whole milk, warmed with an onion studded with 8 cloves
· 100g mature Cheddar, grated, plus extra for scattering
· Handful of freshly chopped coriander

SHIRO MISO UDON MUSHROOM *and* KALE CARBONARA

This border-blending carbonara that brings together Japan and Italy on one plate is compulsive eating. The miso is emulsified with the egg yolks and Parmesan cheese so it clings and brings a double umami to every strand of noodle. I love the chewy girth of an udon but this recipe also works well with regular spaghetti or bucatini too.

―――――――

Whisk together the egg yolks, Parmesan and miso in a bowl and season with salt (not too much as the cheese is already quite salty) and plenty of black pepper.

Heat the oil in a hot frying pan over medium-high heat and fry the mushrooms for 5 minutes or till nutty and golden, then add the garlic and fry for a minute or two till fragrant. Remove the mushrooms from the pan with a slotted spoon and set aside and then in the same pan sauté the kale for 3 minutes or until wilted. Remove the pan from the heat.

Cook the udon noodles according to packet instructions. Drain, reserving a cupful of the cooking water. Add the drained noodles to the pan with the kale and toss the mushrooms back in.

Whisk a little of the cooking water into the egg yolk mixture – this will help temper the eggs and prevent them from scrambling. Pour the egg yolk mixture over the udon noodles and toss and stir to combine – the heat from the noodles will cook the egg, forming a thick sauce. Drizzle in a little more cooking liquid if you need to thin it out a bit, but it should be lovely and glossy, coating the noodles. Stir in the chopped spring onion greens and serve with a scattering of togarashi and extra Parmesan if desired.

· 4 egg yolks
· 60g grated Parmesan or pecorino Romano cheese, plus extra to serve
· 1 heaped tbsp shiro miso
· 1 tbsp olive oil
· 250g chestnut mushrooms, thickly sliced
· 2 garlic cloves, finely chopped
· 100g kale, roughly torn and tough ribs discarded
· 200g udon noodles
· 2 spring onions, green parts only, thinly sliced
· Sea salt and freshly ground black pepper
· Togarashi, to serve

AROMATIC COCONUT, PUMPKIN *and* GREEN BEAN RICE NOODLE BOWLS

At the top of my list of satisfying meals that nurture body and soul is a big, steaming bowl of noodles in broth. The broth here is based on a Keralan ishtew – a coastal curry cooked with aromatic whole spices and coconut milk. It's so rich with the flavour of coconut that it tastes like a vacation in a bowl. Slurping the rice noodles noisily and then clearing the dregs of the broth straight from the bowl may not be polite but it is happy making!

———————

Preheat the oven to 200°C/Fan 180°C/Gas Mark 6. Arrange the wedges of pumpkin or squash on a baking tray, drizzle with oil and season with salt and pepper. Roast for 30 minutes until golden and caramelised then set side.

Bring a saucepan of salted water to a rolling boil and blanch the green beans for 2 minutes, then drain and refresh in ice-cold water. Drain and set aside.

Now to make the ishtew. Heat the oil in a large saucepan over medium-high heat and, once hot, add the cinnamon, star anise, cloves, cardamom and peppercorns. Fry briefly till fragrant then add the curry leaves and chillies and fry again for a minute till fragrant. Scatter in the onions and fry over low-medium heat for 8 minutes till soft and translucent, then add the ginger and garlic and fry for 2–3 minutes till fragrant. Pour in the coconut milk and the water, season and bring to the boil. Reduce the heat and simmer for 8–10 minutes to let the flavours deepen. Season with salt and pepper.

When you are ready to serve, gently warm the pumpkin or squash through the sauce, add the green beans for 30 seconds, then take off the heat. Add the coriander and lime juice and stir.

Divide the noodles among bowls then add the pumpkin or squash and green beans with the sauce. Garnish with cashews, chilli and ginger and serve hot.

- 1kg pumpkin or butternut squash, peeled, deseeded and cut into wedges
- 250g green beans, trimmed
- Sea salt and black pepper
- Rapeseed oil to drizzle

FOR THE ISHTEW
- 2 tbsp coconut oil
- 1 cinnamon stick
- 1 star anise
- 3 cloves
- 5 green cardamom pods, bruised
- ¼ tsp black peppercorns
- 15 fresh curry leaves
- 2 green chillies, slit lengthways
- 2 onions, very thinly sliced
- Thumb of ginger, peeled and finely julienned
- 3 garlic cloves, thinly sliced
- 400ml coconut milk
- 100ml water
- Handful of finely chopped coriander
- Juice of 1 lime

TO SERVE
- 300g fresh rice noodles
- Large handful of toasted cashews
- 1 red chilli, thinly sliced on the diagonal
- 3cm piece of ginger, peeled and finely julienned

SWEET *and* SOUR DHAL *with* CHICKPEA FLOUR PASTA RAGS

148

There is comfort food that comforts, then there is comfort food that soothes the soul – there is also comfort food like this one-pot Gujarati dish commonly known as Dhal Dhokli that brings pure joy. It combines two of my favourite things – pasta and dhal. Making the diamond-shaped pasta is no chore if you have a rolling pin and a knife.

————

To make the pasta dough, mix together all the ingredients in a bowl, then slowly add just enough (about 100ml) lukewarm water to knead a soft, pliable dough – it should not be sticky, so add a little more chapatti flour if it is too wet. Divide the dough into 4 equal balls. Dust the surface with chapatti flour, then roll each ball out into thin rounds about 2mm thick. Cut into 2cm-wide strips, then cut the strips into diamond shapes. Set aside.

To make the dhal, bring the lentils, chilli, turmeric and peanuts to the boil in a saucepan with plenty of water, then reduce the heat to low and simmer for 45 minutes until soft and mushy.

In a separate pan, make the tempering. Heat the ghee, then add the mustard seeds. As soon as they start to pop, add the asafoetida followed by the curry leaves. Once the leaves are crackling, add the Kashmiri chilli, cumin, cinnamon, cloves and fry briefly before adding the ginger, garlic and chillies. Fry for 3 minutes until cooked and fragrant, then add the tomato puree, passata, tamarind and jaggery. Let it come to a bubble and simmer for 5 minutes. Pour into the cooked lentils along with some water to make a soupy dhal and cook for 15 minutes.

To serve, add the dhokli to the dhal and simmer gently for 15 minutes until the dhokli are cooked. Add the lime juice and sprinkle with coriander and red onion to serve.

FOR THE PASTA/DHOKLI DOUGH
· 125g chakki atta (white chapatti flour), plus extra for dusting
· 2 tbsp chickpea (gram) flour
· 1 tsp red chilli powder
· ½ tsp ground turmeric
· ½ tsp ajwain or carom seeds
· 1 tbsp rapeseed oil
· ½ tsp sea salt

FOR THE DHAL
· 200g oily toor dhal
· 1 long red chilli, cut into thick rings
· 1 tsp ground turmeric
· Handful of raw skinned peanuts

FOR THE TEMPERING
· 2 tbsp ghee
· 1 heaped tsp brown mustard seeds
· Pinch of asafoetida
· 15–20 fresh curry leaves
· 1 Kashmiri chilli, broken up
· 1 tsp cumin seeds
· 1 cinnamon stick, broken up
· 2 cloves
· 1 tbsp grated ginger
· 3 garlic cloves, blitzed
· 2 green chillies, finely blitzed
· 1 heaped tsp tomato puree
· 100g passata
· 1 tbsp tamarind paste
· 2 tbsp grated jaggery or soft brown sugar
· Juice of 1 lime

TO GARNISH
· 3 tbsp finely chopped coriander
· 2 tbsp finely chopped red onion

BRAISED MUSHROOM NOODLES

This dish is like fungi porn. It's an orgy for a multitude of mushroom species: shiitakes that look like toasted marshmallows, field mushrooms with rosy open gills, alien enoki, phallic king oysters, feathery hen of the woods and chanterelles like flimsy golden parasols. Mushrooms are tenacious enough to stand up to the boldest seasonings and burst with their own unique meaty juices which they release with little encouragement. They make great sponges for the delicious sauce made with soy, ginger and garlic. It's like a mushroom ragu with an Asian slant and is wonderful with springy egg noodles.

Prepare the noodles according to packet instructions and set aside. Drain the porcini mushrooms, squeeze out excess liquid and roughly chop.

Heat the oil in a wok over medium-high heat. Add the garlic and ginger and stir-fry for a couple of minutes until fragrant. Add the sliced mushrooms and stir-fry for 4–5 minutes until nutty brown then add the mirin, soy sauces, sugar and stock. Bring to the boil, then slowly pour in the cornflour water and stir and cook till the sauce is glossy and thickened. Add the porcini and noodles and stir gently to prevent the noodles from breaking up. As soon as the noodles come to the boil, add the sesame oil and spring onion. Serve scattered with sesame seeds.

- 250g dried egg noodles
- 2 tbsp dried porcini mushrooms, soaked in just-boiled water for 10 minutes
- 2 tbsp rapeseed oil
- 3 garlic cloves, finely chopped
- Thumb of ginger, peeled and julienned
- 500g mixed mushrooms, thickly sliced – I love oyster, king oyster, chanterelles, shiitake, enoki
- 1 tbsp mirin
- 1 tbsp light soy sauce
- 1 tsp dark soy sauce
- ½ tsp caster sugar
- 400ml good-quality vegetable stock
- 1 tsp cornflour, dissolved in a little cold water
- A few drops of toasted sesame oil
- 1 spring onion, trimmed and finely julienned
- Toasted white sesame seeds, to garnish

SOBA NOODLES *with* CABBAGE, BRUSSELS SPROUTS *and* ALMOND BUTTER DRESSING

I love that soba noodles can be served cold, making them ideal for leftovers and lunchboxes. The idea with this salad is texture, so use whatever raw vegetables you have to hand – carrots, mangetout and peppers all work well. The dressing is addictive – I love almond butter, but you can equally use peanut or cashew butter or even tahini; it is highly riffable.

––––––––––

First make the dressing. Heat the oil in a small saucepan over low heat, add the shallot and fry gently for 10 minutes till caramelised. Add the garlic, chilli and lime zest and sauté for a couple of minutes till fragrant then transfer to a food processor. Add the remaining ingredients and process until smooth.

In a large bowl, mix together the noodles, cabbage, Brussels, edamame, kale and spring onions and drizzle with some of the dressing, then top with toasted almonds and coriander and serve along with the remaining dressing.

· 225g soba noodles, cooked according to packet instructions and drained
· ½ small red cabbage, thinly sliced
· 200g Brussels sprouts, finely shredded
· 100g edamame beans
· 100g kale, finely shredded
· 2 spring onions, thinly sliced (including green parts)

FOR THE DRESSING
· 1 tbsp rapeseed oil
· 1 banana shallot, very finely chopped
· 2 garlic cloves, very finely chopped
· 1 small red chilli, finely chopped
· Zest and juice of 2 limes
· 400ml coconut cream
· 150g blanched almonds
· 2 tbsp tamari or light soy sauce
· 1 tbsp maple syrup
· 1 tbsp tamarind concentrate

TO SERVE
· Toasted flaked or chopped almonds
· Handful of roughly chopped coriander

COLD KELP NOODLES
with SILKEN TOFU *and*
BLACK VINEGAR DRESSING

Kelp noodles are an inexpensive staple I always have in my pantry to add low-calorie heft to salads and broths. They can simply be rinsed and eaten – no cooking required – and have a wonderful refreshing and crunchy texture. They are neutral enough to take on assertive flavours, too. This is the perfect recipe for a heatwave as it doesn't require you to turn on the hob and comes together in just 10 minutes.

———————

Make the dressing by simply whisking together all the ingredients in a bowl.

Lay the kelp noodles in a serving bowl and top with the slices of tofu. Pour over the dressing and top with spring onion, peanuts, crisp-fried shallots and cress. Serve.

- 200g kelp noodles, washed and drained well
- 300g gold-quality silken tofu, cut into 1.5cm-thick slices
- 1 spring onion, thinly sliced
- 25g roasted unsalted peanuts, roughly chopped
- Crisp-fried shallots
- Asian cress, to garnish

FOR THE BLACK
VINEGAR DRESSING
- 30ml Chinese chilli oil
- ½ tsp Sichuan peppercorns, roughly crushed
- 1½ tbsp light soy sauce
- 3 tsp Chiankiang vinegar
- 3 tsp Shaoxing rice wine
- 1½ tsp rice vinegar
- 1½ tsp peeled and finely grated ginger
- 1 tsp caster sugar

7
CURRIES
AND
STEWS

AN
EDUCATION

The earthy perfume of cumin roasting on a hot, arid pan. The fragrance of mustard seeds and curry leaves blooming in ghee. These are the familiar scents that let me know that I've come home. This is my mother's kitchen, her country and territory. It is the aroma of individual vegetable dishes we reductively refer to as 'curries' bubbling on the stove, drawing me into the centre. Somewhere in England, this is an outpost of the homeland. These dishes are memory, colour and nostalgia captured in heavy stainless-steel cooking pots.

There are baby pumpkins tinted yellow with turmeric softening in a ginger and tomato sauce. 'Pay attention,' my mother would say when I was young. 'Someday you'll need to know all of this.' The scent of sweet earthy turnips laced with Bengali five-spice wafts in memories of coming home after school and getting to have the first taste in a small brass bowl. 'Someday, I'll give you my secret recipe,' she would say.

My mother's kitchen had always held a fascination for me that deepened when we suddenly left Kenya and found ourselves in blustery England. The sliver of the identity I wanted to recapture, who I really was when I wasn't struggling with a growing divided identity, lay not in schoolbooks or my few new friends, but in my mother's masala jars and cooking paraphernalia. Here I found a place where I felt connected to home.

Mum was a stern teacher – all gnashing teeth and tongs. She
reproached and disapproved, tutted and harrumphed and lost her
temper frequently, but her curries were superlative, so it was worth
it. I can't describe the overwhelming joy and sense of achievement
that came when she gave a stiff nod of approval to okra stewed with
onions, tomatoes and potatoes that I had made without her aid. She
was well respected in our community and often invited to cook at
weddings or religious festivals. She had that intangible energy special
people possess that makes their meals not only good, but exceptional –
a brilliance that stretches beyond the physical attributes of a dish.

What made her curries exemplary was the interplay between her and
the ingredients – the secret magic she could impart to even the most
inanimate potato. It was about the time and energy she spent selecting
and preparing everything from the right sort of onion and how it
was to be cut to the type of chilli – fresh, dry, powdered or whole?
Her innate knowledge and perception was extraordinary, her nose
like a prized bloodhound acutely tuned in to the steroidal potency
of spices – knowing intuitively when to keep them whole or when
to pound them into a fine powder. She tore around the kitchen and
flavours blossomed in her dexterous hands. Her dishes were presented
beautifully and generously but above all she cooked with an intent to
nurture and nourish. It was the only way she knew how to express her
strange, mute love.

My mother is older now. Her mind is still sharp but her body won't
keep up, so she has had to step back a little from her kitchen.
Abdication for a woman as opinionated in culinary matters as she is
must not be easy. I wonder how she rates my versions of her dishes
and I seek her approval still. I am grateful for the gift she shared with
me; the numerous unwritten recipes, cryptic instructions, the nifty
tips and the tricks – an inheritance, an imprinting of the tongue.
I hope she sees what I am made of, how much I am made like her.

JERUSALEM ARTICHOKE *and* CARROT SCHNITZEL KATSU CURRY

Katsu, a popular Japanese comfort food of breaded cutlets, is commonly made with chicken or pork. For my vegan version, I have used Jerusalem artichokes and carrots because they have a natural sweetness and hold their shape when fried. They are dredged in flour, egg and panko breadcrumbs, then fried until golden brown for an irresistible crispy crust. The pea shoot salad brings freshness to the whole dish. Serve with sticky rice.

· 4 large Jerusalem artichokes, halved lengthways
· 4 large carrots, halved lengthways
· 125g plain flour
· 3 eggs, beaten
· 200g panko breadcrumbs
· 500g chanterelle mushrooms
· 50g butter
· 200ml rapeseed oil, for frying
· Sea salt and black pepper

FOR THE KATSU SAUCE
· 2 tbsp rapeseed oil
· 1 onion, thinly sliced
· ½ Bramley apple, peeled and grated
· Thumb of ginger, peeled and finely grated
· 2 garlic cloves, finely chopped
· 2½ tbsp katsu curry or Madras curry powder
· 3 tbsp plain flour
· 600ml water
· 60ml light soy sauce
· 2 tsp honey
· 2 tsp rice vinegar

FOR THE PEA SHOOT SALAD
· 2 tsp light soy sauce
· 1½ tsp rice vinegar
· 1 tsp toasted sesame oil
· 100g pea shoots
· 4 spring onions, sliced into thin 4cm lengths

Parboil the halved Jerusalem artichokes and carrots in a saucepan with plenty of salted boiling water for 15 minutes, then drain and leave to cool.

Place the flour, beaten eggs and panko breadcrumbs in separate bowls. Line an oven tray with baking paper. Dredge the artichokes and carrots evenly in flour, shaking off the excess, then dip into the egg. Ensure they are completely covered, then press into the crumbs, coating evenly. Transfer to the lined tray and set aside until you are ready to fry.

For the katsu sauce, heat the oil in a saucepan over low-medium heat, add the onion and fry slowly for 8 minutes till it is lightly caramelised. Next, add the apple and cook for 5–6 minutes till it has broken down, then add the ginger and garlic and sauté for a couple of minutes until fragrant. Add the curry powder, stir till fragrant, then stir in the flour and cook for 3–4 minutes until sandy and light golden. Gradually whisk in the water, then add the soy sauce and honey and simmer, whisking occasionally, for about 10 minutes and then add the rice vinegar. Remove from the heat and set aside. Once cool, blend into a puree in a processor until smooth and then, if you want a silken sauce, pass it through a sieve.

For the mushrooms, melt the butter in a frying pan over medium-high heat. When foaming, add the mushrooms and fry for 5 minutes until

brown and nutty. Season well with salt and pepper. Remove from the heat and set aside.

For the pea shoot salad, whisk together the soy sauce, rice vinegar and sesame oil and mix with pea shoots and spring onions.

Heat the rapeseed oil in a frying pan over medium-high heat, and once hot, fry the carrots and artichokes in batches for 5–6 minutes, turning them once until they are golden brown and crisp. Drain on a plate lined with kitchen paper. Spoon the katsu sauce into the base of a bowl and lay over carrots, artichokes and mushrooms and serve with a pile of pea shoot salad. Serve immediately.

PICKLED POTATO CURRY

This moreishly sticky curry has both the bolshy heat of chilli and the sweetness of jaggery. If you can't get hold of jaggery, try using soft brown sugar instead. Roasting and flattening the potatoes will give you lovely crisp crevices, but will also allow the delicious sauce to penetrate the potatoes.

———————

Soak the jaggery with the vinegar in a bowl – mix briefly, then leave to dissolve.

Cook the potatoes in a large saucepan with plenty of salted boiling water until tender, then drain.

Preheat the oven to 220°C/Fan 200°C/Gas Mark 7 then pour the 2 tablespoons of oil for the potatoes into a small, shallow roasting tin and heat it in the oven for 5 minutes.

Crush the potatoes with the back of a spoon or bowl so they split open slightly but don't fall apart – this will help them crisp up, but also allow the pickle sauce to penetrate them. Roast for 30 minutes, turning them halfway so they are crisp and golden brown all over.

When the potatoes are almost ready, heat the oil for the pickle sauce in a large frying pan over medium heat. Once hot, add the star anise, cardamom, ginger and garlic and fry for a minute or two until golden and fragrant then sprinkle in the cinnamon. Once it is aromatic, pour in the jaggery and vinegar and cook over medium heat for 3–4 minutes until it's golden and bubbling and most of the vinegar has evaporated. Sprinkle in the chilli flakes and season, mix once, then throw in the roasted potatoes and coat them in the sticky spicy sauce. Finish with coriander and sesame seeds and serve at once.

- 750g small new potatoes
- 2 tbsp rapeseed oil

FOR THE PICKLE SAUCE
- 200g jaggery, grated
- 6 tbsp white wine vinegar
- 2 tbsp rapeseed oil
- 1 star anise
- 1 black cardamom pod, bruised
- Thumb of ginger, peeled and finely grated
- 4 garlic cloves, finely chopped
- ½ tsp ground cinnamon
- ½ tsp dried chilli flakes
- 2 tbsp finely chopped coriander
- Toasted white sesame seeds, to garnish
- Sea salt

PUNJABI SHALGAM SAAG
with CHILLI BROWN BUTTER

Turnips have a dowdy reputation, but when cooked like this with spices and polenta, provide a sweet uncomplicated pleasure that is very underrated. This turnip saag comes from Punjab – it's an archaic dish that is rarely cooked outside the homes of our elders, but it is one that I think is worth preserving. Eat this with puffs of chapatti, slabs of cornbread, or swap it out for mashed potatoes when you are next looking for a starchy side.

———————

Place the turnips in a heavy-based saucepan along with some salt, the turmeric and the water. Cover, bring to the boil, then reduce the heat to low and simmer for 20 minutes till very tender. Crush down with a potato masher – you can go smooth or chunky – I sometimes go in with a stick blender to make it completely smooth but it's lovely either way. Add the polenta, a little at a time, and continue to cook, stirring continuously, for about 15 minutes until the raw flavour has cooked out.

In a frying pan, heat the ghee over low heat, add the onion and paanch phoran and sauté for 15 minutes until caramelised. Blend the ginger, garlic and chilli in a blender to make a fine paste then add to the pan and cook for 2–3 minutes till soft and fragrant. Add the tomato puree and passata and season with salt and the sugar. Cook for 8 minutes or until jammy then pour the mixture into the cooked turnips. Put the turnips back over low heat, stir and cook for another 10 minutes.

To make the chilli brown butter, melt the butter in a small saucepan over medium heat for a minute or two, till it starts to foam and turn golden brown, stir in the Turkish pepper flakes then take off the heat and pour over the cooked turnips. Scatter over the coriander and serve hot.

· 1kg turnips, diced
· ½ tsp ground turmeric
· 350ml water
· 75g fine polenta or cornmeal
· 2 tbsp ghee
· 1 red onion, very finely chopped
· 1 tsp paanch phoran
· Thumb of ginger
· 2 garlic cloves
· 1 green chilli
· 1 tbsp tomato puree
· 100g passata
· 2 tbsp light brown sugar
· Handful of finely chopped coriander
· Sea salt

FOR THE CHILLI BROWN BUTTER
· 50g unsalted butter
· 1 tsp Turkish pepper flakes (pul biber)

MANGO *and* GOLDEN COIN CURRY

Mangoes in the summer are so saturated with rapture and nostalgia. This curry where they are served whole really captures their joy – not slicing them feels generous and luxuriant. Serve them with puris or chapattis to scrape the sumptuous flesh off the stone; sucking the remnants from the stone is fine in polite company, too. The heat from the spices, sourness from the tamarind and lush sweetness from the mango makes for a balanced, surprising and addictive curry. The 'golden coins' are little gram flour dumplings that give you something to get your teeth into.

———————

First, make the golden coins. Sift the chickpea (gram) flour into a large bowl and add the spices and salt. Pour in the oil and yoghurt and rub through the flour, making sure it is well incorporated. Add the water a little at a time and knead for 7–8 minutes until you have a smooth, soft and pliable dough.

Bring a large pot of water to the boil. Divide the dough into six equal parts. Roll each part to a smooth ball and then roll into a cylindrical sausage shape about 2cm thick. Gently place each cylinder in the boiling water. Don't overcrowd the pan – cook in batches if necessary. After they are cooked, the cylinders will float to the surface and should be bubbled on the surface – this will take roughly 5 minutes. Gently remove them with a slotted spoon and drain on a clean tea towel to soak up excess water. Place them on a chopping board and cool and then slice 5mm-thick discs from them. Set aside.

Now for the mango curry. Wash the mangoes thoroughly and peel. Set the peeled mangoes aside, then use a small, sharp knife to scrape all the residual pulp from the skin into a bowl and puree. Puree the flesh from 2 of the mangoes with 100ml water, stir to combine and set aside.

In a blender, grind the coriander and sesame seeds to a coarse powder. Add the drained soaked chillies, sugar, coconut and

- 6 ripe mangoes, such as alphonso or kesar
- 1 tsp coriander seeds, toasted
- 1 tbsp white sesame seeds, toasted
- 6 hot dried red chillies, soaked in 50ml hot water for 1 hour
- 1 tbsp grated jaggery or light brown sugar
- 80g fresh grated coconut
- 65g tamarind paste
- 2 tbsp rapeseed oil
- 1 tsp brown mustard seeds
- Pinch of asafoetida
- 15 fresh curry leaves
- 1 long red chilli, sliced into thick rings
- ½ tsp ground turmeric
- Sea salt
- Freshly chopped coriander, to garnish

FOR THE GOLDEN COINS
- 200g chickpea (gram) flour
- Pinch of asafoetida
- ¼ tsp ground turmeric
- ½ tsp ajwain or carom seeds
- ½ tsp red chilli powder
- 1 tsp ground coriander
- ½ tsp sea salt
- 3 tbsp rapeseed oil
- 2 tbsp natural yoghurt
- 4–5 tbsp water

168

tamarind, and blend to a smooth paste. Add a little water to loosen, if needed.

Heat the oil in a large saucepan over high heat and, once it's good and hot, sprinkle in the mustard seeds. As soon as they crackle, add the asafoetida, curry leaves and chilli, and fry for 1 minute until fragrant. Reduce the heat to low-medium, stir in the turmeric, then add the coconut paste and fry for 5 minutes or until aromatic. Pour in the reserved mango pulp mix, add the whole peeled fruit and golden coins, season with sea salt and stir gently, spooning the sauce over the fruit. Cover and cook for 10–15 minutes, turning the mangoes once halfway. Uncover the pan, cook for a further few minutes, then garnish with coriander and serve.

BABY AUBERGINES *and* NEW POTATOES COOKED IN A SWEET AND SOUR NUT PASTE

170

Baby aubergines are one of my favourite ingredients for curries. They cook quickly and look cute, but more than that, they are like little sponges for flavour. In this case that flavour comes from a sauce that is luxuriant with a paste made from coconut and nuts and sour tamarind to cut through all that richness. This recipe is a keeper – one that you will come back to time after time.

———

Cook the potatoes in a pan of salted boiling water till tender then drain.

Preheat the oven to 200°C/Fan 180°C/Gas Mark 6. Quarter the aubergines lengthways but don't go all the way through the stem – you still want to keep the aubergine attached and intact. Lay them on a roasting tray along with potatoes. Season with a little salt, drizzle over some rapeseed oil and roast for 20 minutes until the aubergines are tender and the potatoes are golden.

To make the nut paste, toast the sesame seeds, poppy seeds, coriander seeds and fennel seeds in a hot dry frying pan for a minute or two and then blitz in a spice grinder or food processor to make a coarse powder. Add the nuts and coconut and grind again till it's as fine as you can get it.

Next, heat the rapeseed oil in a frying pan over low heat, add the onion and fry for 10–15 minutes till caramelised. Add the onion, along with the tamarind, sugar and chilli powder to the blender with the ground nuts and blend to a thick paste.

Heat the oil for tempering the spices in the frying pan over medium-high heat. Add the paanch phoran and, once the spices crackle, add the curry leaves and fry for 15 seconds, then add the garlic and chilli. Fry for 1 minute until fragrant. Now spoon the nut paste into the frying pan, thin down with a little water and then add the aubergines and potatoes. Cover and simmer over low heat for 10 minutes. Serve strewn with picked coriander leaves.

· 500g baby new potatoes
· 8 baby aubergines
· Rapeseed oil, for drizzling
· Sea salt
· Picked coriander leaves, to garnish

FOR THE NUT PASTE
· 2 tbsp white sesame seeds
· 1 tbsp white poppy seeds
· 1 tbsp coriander seeds
· 1 tbsp fennel seeds
· 50g peanuts, toasted
· 50g cashew nuts, toasted
· 100g fresh grated coconut
· 1 tbsp rapeseed oil
· 1 onion, sliced
· 2 tbsp tamarind paste
· 1 tbsp grated jaggery or light brown sugar
· 1 tsp Kashmiri chilli powder

FOR THE TEMPERING
· 2 tbsp rapeseed oil
· 1 tsp paanch phoran
· 15–20 fresh curry leaves
· 3 garlic cloves, finely chopped
· 1 long red chilli, thinly sliced on the diagonal

PANEER BRAISED *in* KALE, SPINACH *and* SORREL

This is my take on saag paneer – a hearty dish where greens are stewed with ginger, garlic and chilli before nuggets of soft paneer are tossed in. I have used a combination of spinach, kale and sorrel for Popeye-pleasing amounts of goodness, but you could just as well use just spinach or any combination of other greens such as chard, dandelion or collard greens. Serve with paratha, chapati or a flatbread of your choice.

————

Bring a large pan of salted water to the boil. Drop in the paneer and boil for 5 minutes and then fish it out with a slotted spoon. Blanch the spinach, kale and sorrel in the boiling water for 30 seconds then refresh in ice-cold water. Squeeze out excess water from the greens, roughly chop and puree in a blender till smooth.

Heat the ghee in a large heavy-based pan over low heat, add the onion along with the cumin seeds and fry for 15 minutes until caramelised. Add the garlic, ginger and chilli and fry for 2–3 minutes till fragrant, then add the passata and turmeric and cook for 5 minutes. Fold in the pureed greens and continue to cook for 5 minutes before folding in the paneer and seasoning with salt. Cover the pan and let the paneer cook over low heat for 10 minutes. Serve with chapati or naan or any other flatbread your heart desires.

- 300g paneer, cubed
- 500g fresh spinach, well washed
- 250g kale
- 200g sorrel
- 2 tbsp ghee
- 1 onion, very finely chopped
- 1 heaped tsp cumin seeds
- 3 fat garlic cloves, very thinly sliced
- Thumb of ginger, peeled and grated
- 1 fresh small green chilli, finely chopped
- 200g passata
- ½ tsp ground turmeric
- Sea salt

BRAISED PUMPKIN
with TAMARIND, CASHEW NUTS
and COCONUT

174

The sourness of the tamarind works particularly well against the sweetness of the pumpkin here. You can use any variety of squash – from the big guys to smaller butternut or acorn squashes. This makes a dry curry so it's perfect to fill dosas with or serve accompanied by any other Indian bread.

————————

Heat the oil in a large casserole dish over high heat. As soon as it is shimmering hot, scatter in the mustard seeds. As soon as they start to pop and sputter, chase with the asafoetida and curry leaves. Fry briefly for a minute till fragrant then reduce the heat and add the cinnamon, star anise and dried chilli (if using). Fry for 30 seconds then add the ginger and chopped fresh chilli, stir-frying for a minute or two till the ginger is fragrant and cooked. Add the tomatoes, tamarind and jaggery and cook for 3–4 minutes, until the jaggery has dissolved.

Tumble in the pumpkin, season well with salt and stir, making sure the pumpkin is well coated in the sauce. Cover the pan and cook for about 20 minutes over low heat, stirring occasionally until the pumpkin is soft, then add the cashews, cover and cook for another 5 minutes. Finally, scatter over the coconut and stir. Serve hot or at room temperature.

· 1 tbsp coconut oil or rapeseed oil
· 1 tsp brown mustard seeds
· Pinch of asafoetida
· 15 fresh curry leaves
· 1 cinnamon stick, broken up
· 1 star anise
· 1 dried red Kashmiri chilli, broken – optional
· 30g peeled and grated ginger
· 1 long red chilli, finely chopped
· 200g tinned chopped tomatoes, roughly smashed
· 2 tbsp tamarind concentrate
· 1 tbsp grated jaggery or light brown sugar
· 750g pumpkin or squash, peeled and cubed
· Generous handful of cashews, toasted
· Handful of toasted unsweetened desiccated coconut
· Sea salt

YELLOW TOFU *and* PINEAPPLE CURRY

A curry paste made with the sweet sourness of pineapple is the central flavour of this wonderfully nourishing curry. Coconut milk lends a subtle creaminess and carries the big flavours that are soaked up by the tofu. The pineapple and mangetout bring bright, pleasing bursts of freshness. Serve topped with plenty of fresh Thai basil.

———————

First, make the curry paste. Drain the chillies then pound them in a heavy stone pestle and mortar until you have a smooth paste, then add the bird's eye chilli, turmeric and garlic and pound again. Add the lemongrass stalks and shallot and continue to pound until smooth, then finally add the roughly chopped pineapple and pound again. You could do this all in a food processor if you don't fancy the workout!

Mix the stock and curry paste together in a saucepan and bring to the boil then reduce the heat to low and simmer over low heat for 15 minutes. Add the tofu and pineapple chunks, cover and cook for 5 minutes or until the pineapple is tender, then add the mangetout. Add the soy sauce and tamarind, sprinkle in the sugar and stir to combine. Cook for another 5 minutes, then remove from the heat and finish with lime juice and torn Thai basil and serve with sticky rice.

- 500ml vegetable stock
- 280g firm tofu, cubed
- 200g pineapple, cut into chunks
- 100g mangetout
- 3 tbsp light soy sauce
- 3 tbsp tamarind paste
- 1 tbsp grated palm sugar or soft brown sugar
- Lime juice, to taste
  Thai basil leaves, to serve

FOR THE CURRY PASTE
- 3 dried red chillies, soaked in hot water for 30 minutes
- 1 red bird's eye chilli
- 2cm piece of fresh turmeric
- 3 garlic cloves
- 2 lemongrass stalks
- 1 banana shallot
- 100g roughly chopped pineapple

LOVE ME NOT

SWEET *and* SOUR STUFFED OKRA FRY

178

This is a take on a dish that our Gujarati neighbours in Nairobi frequently cooked. Okra are slit and deftly stuffed with a chunky spice paste, a complexly-flavoured mixture of crushed peanuts, tamarind, chickpea (gram) flour and spices. As they cook, the stuffing melts into a sticky, irresistible sauce. I like to serve this with a simple dhal and some chapatis.

———

Wipe the okra with a damp cloth to clean them and get rid of any grit and set aside.

In a blender, whizz together the sesame and coriander seeds to make a powder then add the peanuts and grind again. Empty into a large bowl. Wipe out the blender then whizz together the green chilli and ginger till finely ground and empty into the bowl with the seeds and peanuts.

Toast the chickpea (gram) flour in a large dry frying pan over medium heat for 4–5 minutes, stirring occasionally, till it is lovely and toasty. Add to the ground peanut mix. Sprinkle in the chilli powder, salt (to taste), turmeric and jaggery and mix, then add the tamarind and season and mix again. You should have a thick, coarse paste.

Make a deep slit on one side of each piece of okra and stuff with as much of the paste as you can get in. Heat the rapeseed oil in a wide, shallow pan over low-medium heat. Add the cumin seeds and when they crackle add the asafoetida, then lay the okra in the pan, stuffing side up, sprinkle over a little more salt, cover and cook for about 5 minutes, turn once, cover and cook for another 5 minutes. Squeeze over lime juice, then sprinkle over the coconut and serve.

- 350g okra
- 2 tsp toasted white sesame seeds
- 1 tbsp toasted coriander seeds
- 4 tbsp unsalted peanuts
- 1 green chilli, roughly chopped
- 3cm piece of ginger, peeled and roughly chopped
- 50g chickpea (gram) flour
- 1 tsp red chilli powder
- ¼ tsp ground turmeric
- 2 tbsp grated jaggery or soft brown sugar
- 2 tbsp tamarind paste
- 4 tbsp rapeseed oil
- 2 tsp cumin seeds
- Pinch of asafoetida
- Lime juice, to taste
- Sea salt
- 1 tbsp grated fresh coconut, to garnish

VEGAN COURGETTE *and* SPINACH KOFTA MAKHANI

This is a vegan take on a wildly luxurious murgh makhani or butter chicken. Rather than chicken there are 'meatballs' made of grated courgette and spinach. The sauce skips the traditional butter and cream and relies on nut butter and vegan coconut yoghurt for richness instead. It is a curry I get asked to make by friends regularly. The same sauce is also excellent with chunks of tofu or fried baby aubergines.

———

Begin by making the courgette and spinach koftas. Put the grated courgettes in a colander, sprinkle with the salt and leave for 30 minutes. Squeeze out as much water from them as possible, pat them dry and put in a large bowl.

Blanche the spinach in boiling water for 20 seconds and refresh in ice-cold water. Drain and squeeze out excess moisture then finely chop and mix with the courgettes. Add all the remaining ingredients (except the oil) and season and mix well.

Heat the oil in a deep, heavy-based saucepan (no more than half full) to 180°C – if you don't have a thermometer, you will know the oil is ready when a cube of bread added to the pan turns golden in 20 seconds. Line a plate with kitchen paper. Form the courgette mix into 12 neat balls (about 25g each) and deep fry in batches for 2 minutes or until they are a rich brown colour. Drain on kitchen paper and set aside while you make the makhani sauce.

Heat the coconut oil in a large saucepan over high heat. Once hot, add the cumin seeds. When they sizzle add the cardamom, cinnamon, bay leaf and peppercorns. Fry briefly then add the onion and cook over low heat for 20 minutes till caramelised. Next, add the ginger, garlic and chilli and sauté till golden, then add the ground coriander, turmeric and Kashmiri chilli powder. Fry for 30 seconds, pour in the passata and nut butter and mix well.

FOR THE KOFTAS
- 500g courgettes, grated
- ½ tsp sea salt
- 100g spinach
- 1 small onion, grated
- 1 green chilli, very finely chopped
- 2.5cm piece of ginger, peeled and finely grated
- 2 tbsp freshly chopped coriander
- 1 tsp fennel seeds, toasted and crushed
- 1 tsp coriander seeds, toasted and crushed
- 1 tbsp unsweetened almond or cashew butter
- 50g chickpea (gram) flour
- Rapeseed oil, for deep frying

FOR THE MAKHANI
- 2 tbsp coconut oil
- 1 tsp cumin seeds
- 4 green cardamom pods, bruised
- 1 cinnamon stick
- 1 bay leaf
- A few black peppercorns
- 1 onion, finely chopped
- Thumb of ginger, peeled and grated
- 3 garlic cloves, very finely chopped
- 1 green chilli, very finely chopped
- 1 heaped tsp ground coriander
- 1 tsp ground turmeric
- 1 tsp Kashmiri chilli powder
- 250g passata
- 4 tbsp unsweetened almond or cashew butter
- 250g coconut yoghurt
- 1 tbsp dried fenugreek (kasoori methi)
- 1 tbsp maple syrup

TO SERVE
- Drizzle of coconut yoghurt
- Handful of freshly chopped coriander

for 8–10 minutes then pour in the yoghurt, season to taste and add the dried fenugreek and maple syrup. Cook over low heat, stirring constantly, for about 5 minutes. Fish out the whole spices and discard, then empty the contents of the pan into a blender and puree till smooth. If desired, pass through a sieve for an extra-smooth sauce. Pour back into the pan, add the courgette and spinach koftas, coat in the sauce and heat till it comes to a gentle simmer. Serve garnished with a drizzle of coconut yoghurt and scattered with coriander.

8
SALADS, VEGETABLES, BAKES AND SIDES

VEGETABLE LITERACY

Kenya, where I was born, is a magical place. Not just because of the spectacular Rift Valley etched against an ever-blue sky, or the lush rolling hills that mark farmland in the highlands, or the endless expanses of acacia trees and tawny savannahs – the people here too have an enduring resilience, warmth and charm. My grandfather went there in the 1940s and fell so deeply in love with the benevolent red soil that he decided to lay down our roots.

My love of vegetables and vegetarian cooking is intertwined with memories of my grandparent's *shaamba*. *Mama* and *Bhaji* were mostly found kneeling on a carpet of soil, tenderly nursing a forest of thriving shrubs. Their allotment was not a shrine to plant prettiness, but it was their small patch of paradise, a temple where sowing, watering and weeding was both a ritual and religion. It was a realm brimming with rebellious greenery; a chartreuse fleece creeping up the ancient whitewashed walls, a bushel of fragrant curry leaves grown from a cutting they had cultivated from the wilds of their native India, shoots of invasive spearmint that colonised every nook, fennel fronds and bishop's weed that tickled the bees, and bright yellow cans of Mazola corn oil resourcefully upcycled into pots for seedlings – their hopeful vertical blades of green pointing skyward as if in prayer.

The soil in Kenya is rich and so, too, are the varieties of vegetables,
fruits and legumes. This abundance suited my grandparents well. Meat
was rarely eaten at home and my grandmother was a strict vegetarian
who had never so much as cracked an egg. Geography and religion
conspired in a way, then, to produce a vegetarian cuisine of surprising
range and ingenuity – one whose infinite variety of flavours was
achieved through the artful combination of ingredients and juggling of
spices. They enjoyed homegrown tomatoes, squashes, baby aubergines
and spinach, but there were indigenous plants too. My grandmother
was talented and wily. She had adapted to the geography of her
adopted African home. She could make sour candies using native
baobab, saag with local greens such as African nightshade or jute, spicy
stews using *maragwe* – a type of local kidney bean – and spicy chips
out of *matoke*, a short local plantain.

My grandparents valued vegetables and fruits to the point of
reverence and wasted nothing. Seeds, peelings, odd and ends were all
repurposed. They came from a generation who were well acquainted
with scarcity and had a deep respect for the invisible chain of
humanity behind every plate of food – the farmers, labourers and
pickers. They understood the fragile magic, love, sacrifice and labour
involved in rearing a seed into something nutritious you could bring
to the table. Our meals were always blessed before we could eat them,
and a prayer of gratitude was always uttered. Sharing the fruits of their
toil with friends and donating it to the lesser privileged was a sort of
consecration.

There are many kinds of infinitely beautiful, complex-flavoured
plants – they are the workhorses of the kitchen and my recipes are
incomplete without them. Like my grandmother, I adore verdant
dishes that invite you to eat your way through a lush garden of them.
This chapter is a celebration of the many ways they can excite your
palate. In our concrete jungles, our lives of windowless offices, growing
them – even if just a few herbs on the windowsill – is critical. It is an
exercise in healing and reconnecting us to our ancestors and gardens,
to nature and our wilder, happier selves.

WATERMELON SALAD *with* PEPPER *and* CASHEW-NUT BRITTLE

Watermelons are social. Their sweet, refreshing flesh invites the company of all manner of flavours and is especially good with a salty component. While feta is the popular choice, I have borrowed from the flavours of Asia here. This salad is a riot of fresh herbs, chilli heat, tamarind sourness and umami soy sauce oomph. Make this and take it to a party – no one will put this baby in the corner.

————

- 1 mini watermelon, roughly cut into bite-sized cubes (rind removed)
- 1 red onion, very thinly sliced into crescents
- Handful of picked coriander leaves
- Handful of picked mint leaves
- Handful of torn Thai basil leaves
- Large handful of crisp-fried shallots
- 1 red chilli, thinly sliced on the diagonal

FOR THE PEPPER AND CASHEW-NUT BRITTLE
- 100g toasted cashew nuts
- ¼ tsp black peppercorns, toasted and roughly ground
- ½ tsp Sichuan peppercorns, toasted and roughly ground
- 150g caster sugar

FOR THE WATERMELON SALAD DRESSING
- 2 fat garlic cloves, roughly chopped
- 1 small red bird's eye chilli, roughly chopped
- 1 tbsp palm sugar or light soft brown sugar
- 50ml pineapple juice
- Juice of ½ lime
- 50ml light soy sauce
- 30g tamarind paste

To make the cashew-nut brittle, spread the cashew nuts on a baking tray lined with baking paper or a silicon baking sheet. Sprinkle over both the ground peppercorns. Cook the sugar in a small saucepan over medium heat without stirring until melted, then bring to the boil and cook until dark caramel in colour. Pour the caramel over the nuts. Leave to stand until cooled and hard, then break into pieces and roughly crush with a mortar and pestle. Set aside in an airtight container.

For the watermelon salad dressing, in a pestle and mortar, pound together the garlic and chilli until you have a paste, then add the sugar, pineapple juice, lime juice, soy sauce and tamarind and stir until the sugar has dissolved.

Toss the watermelon and onion in a bowl and dress liberally with the dressing. Add the herbs and toss to just combine and serve scattered with crisp-fried shallots, cashew brittle and sliced red chilli.

HERITAGE TOMATO SALAD *with* LIME LEAF DRESSING, GINGER *and* CHILLI

Red, yellow, orange, purple and miniature ones as tiny as olives, others gnarled and misshapen like small pumpkins – I am enamoured by the alluring range of tomatoes on offer when they are in season. I carry them home like precious jewels and savour them in simple salads. This one goes well beyond the flavours of the Med. The lime leaf dressing enhances their complex individual flavours, from grassy and vegetal to sweet and tart. Avoid dried lime leaves as they have little to no flavour. You can find fresh lime leaves in most supermarkets now, but I always seek out the bags of frozen ones in Asian supermarkets. They have excellent flavour and are more economical if you are using quite a few. Stash what's left over in your freezer and add them to everything from broths to desserts like panna cotta.

———————

Make the dressing ahead of time so the flavours have time to infuse. Whizz the lime leaves in a powerful blender till they are very finely chopped then drizzle in the oil with the motor still running. Finally add the garlic, soy sauce and lime juice and blend to emulsify.

To make the lime leaf salt, pour the rapeseed oil into a small saucepan so you have a shallow depth of it. Place over high heat and when it's hot and shimmering, quickly fry the lime leaves for a few seconds until they crisp – they will sputter, so stand back. Remove with a slotted spoon, drain on kitchen paper and pat off excess oil. Crumble into a pestle and mortar, add the salt and crush to make a lovely, fragrant green salt.

To serve the salad, arrange the tomatoes on a platter and drizzle over the dressing. Top with a little lime leaf salt, the strips of ginger, sliced chilli, shallot and cress or coriander.

· 500g mixed heritage tomatoes, cut into an assortment of rings, wedges and quarters
· Thumb of ginger, peeled and cut into very fine julienne
· 1 long red chilli, sliced on the diagonal
· 1 banana shallot, very thinly sliced into rounds (use a mandoline if you have one)
· Handful of Asian micro cress – I especially love shiso cress (optional) – or picked coriander leaves

FOR THE LIME LEAF DRESSING
· 10 lime leaves, stalks removed
· 60ml neutral oil
· 1 garlic clove, finely grated
· 30ml light soy sauce
· 30ml lime juice
· ½ tsp caster sugar

FOR THE LIME LEAF SALT
· 60ml rapeseed oil
· 10 lime leaves, stalks removed
· 1 tbsp sea salt

GRILLED PEACHES *with* SILKEN TOFU *and* THAI BASIL *and* LIME LEAF GREMOLATA

The scent of ripe peaches is nostalgic. They smell of languid summer afternoons. In England, peachy perfection is hard to come by because imported fruit is generally picked before it's ripe to prevent it from bruising. As a result, it often goes from hard as a rock to rotten and misses out on that sublime middle stage of ripe sumptuousness. Still, griddling the peaches as I have done for this salad ekes out their natural sweetness and the aniseed notes in the Thai basil and lime leaf gremolata magically makes them taste all the peachier!

————

Begin by making the tofu cream. Pat away the excess liquid from the tofu using kitchen paper. Break it up and place it in a food processor with the rapeseed oil and some sea salt and blend till smooth. Empty into a bowl and set aside.

Clean out the food processor and use it to make the gremolata by simply whizzing together all the ingredients until you have a thick dressing.

Heat a griddle pan over high heat. Drizzle the peaches with a little oil then grill them cut side down in the griddle pan, turning them after 30 seconds or until they have char marks.

To serve the salad, spoon the tofu cream over a plate then lay over the griddled peaches. Drizzle over the gremolata and finally scatter over the red chilli. Serve immediately.

· 300–350g block silken soft tofu
· 1 tbsp cold-pressed rapeseed oil, plus extra for drizzling
· 6 peaches, stoned and cut into wedges
· Sea salt
· 1 long red chilli, sliced thinly on the diagonal, to serve

FOR THE THAI BASIL AND LIME LEAF GREMOLATA
· Small bunch of coriander, including stalks, roughly chopped
· Bunch of Thai basil, leaves torn
· 8 lime leaves, stalks removed, leaves roughly chopped
· 1 bird's eye chilli, roughly chopped
· Grated zest and juice of 1 lime
· 1 tbsp light soy sauce
· 1 tsp soft brown sugar
· 60ml cold-pressed rapeseed oil

CUCUMBER CHAAT *with* LABNEH

Cucumbers belong to the same family as watermelons, and this salad exploits their high water content to make a salad that is perfect for sweltering weather. The dairy dressing is based around the idea of a 'chaas' – a cooling, frothy Indian drink made of salted buttermilk or thin yoghurt spiked with cumin, green chillies, mint and coriander. All in all, it's like a breeze in a bowl.

———

Begin the recipe a day in advance to make the labneh for the dressing. In a small bowl, mix together the yoghurt and a fat pinch of sea salt. Line a bowl with a large square of clean muslin then spoon in the yoghurt. Gather the corners of the muslin and tie together to enclose the yoghurt. Tie to a rack in your fridge and hang, placing the bowl underneath to catch any drips.

The next day, whizz together the chilli, ginger, coriander and mint in a blender, then add the remaining ingredients and blend again. Add a little water if needed. Gently mix into the labneh. Season with sea salt to taste and refrigerate until required.

Using a vegetable peeler, shave the cucumber flesh (including the skin) into long strips, being careful not to include any seeds. Discard the seedy core. Tip the shavings into a colander, sprinkle with salt and the caster sugar, set on a plate and refrigerate for 10 minutes to let some of their liquid leach out. Gently squeeze out any excess liquid then combine with radishes, shallot and pomegranate seeds and toss together.

Smooth the labneh over the surface of serving plate and pile over cucumber strips, radishes and shallots on top. Scatter with crisp noodles and finely chopped coriander and serve.

· 6 Persian cucumbers
· ½ tsp caster sugar
· 10 radishes or 1 large radish, very thinly sliced
· 1 shallot, very thinly sliced
· Seeds from ½ pomegranate
· 100g crisp noodles (sev)
· 2 tbsp finely chopped coriander
· Sea salt

FOR THE LABNEH DRESSING
· 500g Greek yoghurt
· 1 green finger chilli, very finely chopped
· 1 tsp peeled and finely grated ginger
· 1 tbsp freshly chopped coriander
· 1 tbsp freshly chopped mint leaves
· ½ tsp cumin seeds, toasted and coarsely ground
· ¼ tsp chaat masala, or to taste
· ¼ tsp black salt (kala namak) – optional
· 2 tbsp lime juice
· Sea salt

ROASTED BEETROOT *and* BLOOD ORANGE SALAD *with* CURRY LEAF DRESSING

There are slim pickings in winter but there is always the consolation of citrus fruit and earthy beetroots – radiant planets that offer hope, that illuminate and bring consolation to the human spirit with their vivid colour, taste and scent. This beetroot and blood orange salad dressed with the fragrant flavours of a warm South Indian clime will make the grey months less dreary. What's more, all the vitamin C it has packed into it is bound to say boo to your winter flu. Feel free to add a ball of mozzarella or burrata if desired.

––––––––

Preheat the oven to 180°C/Fan 160°C/Gas Mark 4.

Place the beetroots in a roasting tray, fill with 1cm of water and drizzle over a little oil. Season to taste, cover with foil and roast for about 45 minutes, turning the beetroots occasionally, until tender. Once cool, peel and cut the beets into a variety of wedges and rounds and arrange on a platter with the blood oranges. Season with salt and pepper. Sprinkle over the onion, then make the dressing.

Heat the rapeseed oil for the dressing in a small frying pan over high heat. Once it's hot, quickly sprinkle in the mustard seeds. As soon as they start to pop and splutter, chase with a pinch of asafoetida (if using), the curry leaves, chilli and cinnamon. Add the cashews, reduce the heat and stir, letting the cashews colour slightly. Spoon the hot dressing over the salad, scatter over the picked coriander and serve.

· 500g purple beetroots
· 500g yellow beetroots
· Rapeseed oil, for drizzling
· 3 blood oranges, peeled and sliced into rounds
· ½ red onion, very thinly sliced into half moons
· Sea salt and black pepper
· A few picked coriander leaves, to serve

FOR THE CURRY LEAF DRESSING
· 2½ tbsp rapeseed oil
· 1 tsp brown mustard seeds
· Pinch of asafoetida – optional
· 2 stems of fresh curry leaves, picked
· 1 dried red chilli, broken up
· 1 cinnamon stick, broken up
· 2 tbsp cashews

CHARRED MELON *and* TOMATO PANZANELLA

This is a spectacularly refreshing salad, especially when it is made when cantaloupe melons are at their densely honeyed best. You can roast your own peppers or get them out of a jar if you are in a hurry but do make sure your tomatoes are sumptuously ripe. The bread will soften by soaking up all the fruity juices. This is one to make throughout the summer.

———————

Preheat the oven to 200°C/Fan 180°C/Gas Mark 6.

Place the peppers in a roasting tray, drizzle with a little olive oil and roast for 25 minutes or until the skin is dark and blistered, turning them occasionally. Transfer to a bowl, cover with cling film and let them steam for 20 minutes before peeling and tearing into strips. Discard the skin and seeds.

Put the tomatoes in a bowl and scatter with the sugar.

Get a griddle pan nice and hot. Rub the slices of sourdough with the garlic and drizzle with oil. Place the bread on the griddle pan and char on both sides until golden and toasted. Remove from the griddle and once it is cool, tear into chunks and put in the bowl with tomatoes.

Season the melon wedges with salt and pepper and griddle for 2 minutes on each side or until tiger-striped from the griddle. Cool.

Put the red pepper strips, charred melon, onion and capers in the bowl with the tomatoes and bread. Tear in the mozzarella and toss. To make the dressing, shake the oil and vinegar in a jar with some salt and pepper. Pour over the salad and then toss. Add the basil leaves just before serving.

- 3 red peppers
- Olive oil, for drizzling
- 350g mixed baby tomatoes, halved
- 600g ripe tomatoes – try a mixed variety such as oxheart, Vesuvio, Iberiko, etc., cut into a mixture of wedges, quarters and rings
- Fat pinch of caster sugar
- 250g sourdough bread, sliced
- 1 garlic clove
- ½ firm cantaloupe melon, skin and seeds removed, cut into 1cm-thick wedges
- 1 small red onion, thinly sliced
- 2 heaped tbsp capers in vinegar, washed and drained
- 2 balls of buffalo mozzarella
- Small bunch of basil, torn
- Sea salt and black pepper

FOR THE DRESSING
- 100ml extra virgin olive oil
- 60ml red wine vinegar

BROCCOLI, KALE *and* SPINACH KATAIFI PIE

This pie is based on that comforting Greek favourite – spanakopita – although it is far more forgiving to make. There is no buttering and layering of delicate filo pastry: instead, the iron-rich mixture of greens and cheese is blanketed under a nest of buttered kataifi pastry, a shredded filo dough that crisps up beautifully when baked or fried. You'll find kataifi pastry in the fridge or freezer section of Middle Eastern grocers.

Preheat the oven to 180°C/Fan 160°C/Gas Mark 4.

Heat the olive oil in a large pan over low-medium heat, add the onion and sauté for 10 minutes till sweet and caramelised. Add the garlic and fry again till fragrant, then add the kale and soften before adding the spinach. Once the greens are wilted, take off the heat and cool.

Transfer to a large bowl along with the broccoli and add the eggs, pine nuts, currants, feta, ricotta, lemon zest and juice, herbs, nutmeg and sour cream and season with salt and pepper. Mix thoroughly.

Pull apart the strands of kataifi pastry to loosen and fluff them up. Stir the butter through the kataifi, coating it well.

Pour the spinach and ricotta filling into a deep pie dish – I use a 34cm baking dish. Gently pile the kataifi over the pie filling, sprinkle over the sesame seeds and bake for 35–40 minutes, or until the filling is hot and set and the kataifi pastry is golden brown. Serve with a light salad.

- 2 tbsp olive oil
- 1 onion, thinly sliced
- 3 garlic cloves, very finely crushed
- 200g kale, tough ribs removed and leaves roughly chopped
- 200g spinach
- 250g broccoli, boiled till tender and roughly chopped
- 4 eggs
- 60g pine nuts
- 60g currants, golden raisins or barberries
- 250g feta cheese
- 250g ricotta
- Zest of 2 lemons and juice of 1
- Handful of dill, roughly chopped
- Handful of flat-leaf parsley, roughly chopped
- A good grating of nutmeg
- 150g sour cream
- 250g kataifi pastry
- 60g butter, melted
- White sesame seeds, for sprinkling
- Sea salt and black pepper

GUJARATI-STYLE CAVOLO NERO *and* CHICKPEA FLOUR ROTOLO *with* SESAME SEEDS

This takes kale out of the predictable realm of salads, soups and stews. It is my inauthentic take on a favourite Gujarati snack known as patra, which is normally made from rolled colcassia leaves. Those are not the easiest ingredient to come by in the UK, so instead I've used cavolo nero, which has a similarly earthy flavour – you could use savoy or hispi cabbage too. Once you have mastered the art of the layering and rolling technique, it's actually not very hard at all to pull off.

- 16 large cavolo nero leaves

FOR THE PASTE
- 120g tamarind concentrate
- 2 heaped tbsp Greek yoghurt
- 200g chickpea (gram) flour
- 1 tsp red chilli powder
- ½ tsp ground turmeric
- ½ tsp asafoetida
- 2 tbsp grated jaggery or soft brown sugar
- Sea salt, to taste

FOR THE TEMPERING
- 1 tbsp rapeseed oil
- 1 tsp brown mustard seeds
- Pinch of asafoetida
- 1 tsp cumin seeds
- 15 fresh curry leaves
- 1 tbsp white sesame seeds

TO SERVE
- 2 tbsp fresh or frozen grated coconut, defrosted
- 1 tbsp finely chopped coriander

Using a sharp knife or scissors, cut off the tougher part of the cavolo nero stalks, leaving the delicate bit intact, so the leaf holds together.

Mix all the paste ingredients with 80ml water to form a thick, spreadable mixture – if it's too dry, add a little more water, to loosen.

Flatten out the leaves on a work surface bubbly side up – don't be afraid to be quite firm with them to flatten them out. Spread a thin layer of the paste over one. Put another leaf on top and coat that, too, with the paste. Repeat until you have four layers. With the final layer of paste on top, fold in the edges and, starting from the base and rolling towards the tips, roll the leaves together. Make sure the roll is quite tight, then cover the roll with more paste, so it is sealed. Repeat with the remaining leaves and paste, leaving you with four rolls. If you are having trouble keeping them rolled up, secure with a cocktail stick. Line a steamer with baking paper, add the rolls and steam over boiling water for 15 minutes. Leave to cool, then refrigerate for 1 hour, or until firm and set. Gently remove cocktail sticks, if you used them, then cut the rolls into 1cm-thick slices.

To make the tempering, heat the oil in a large frying pan over medium-high heat and add the mustard seeds. When they start to crackle, stir in the asafoetida, cumin and curry leaves, tossing to coat the curry leaves in oil. Reduce the heat, add the sesame seeds, then gently add the cavolo nero rolls in a single layer and fry for 2 minutes on each side until lightly browned. Transfer to a plate, spoon over the spices and oil, sprinkle with the coconut and coriander, and serve.

DAIKON CAKE *with* FRIED GARLIC *and* CHILLI OIL

One of my favourite weekend pastimes is finding a sprawling dim sum mecca. I love the frenetic bustle of people gathered to have a good time amid steaming bamboo trays. I love the usual suspects – plump dumplings and fluffy buns – but I also like to try the more unusual dishes too such as turnip cake which I have discovered is actually made of daikon radish. It is a savoury rice cake made from rice flour and grated daikon, steamed then pan-fried to create a tender texture with a crispy crust. My version excludes the cured pork it normally contains and instead is served with a funky, nutty chilli oil and plenty of crispy fried garlic. Once steamed, the daikon cake can be kept in the fridge for up to about 10 days. Importantly, make sure you make this with non-glutinous rice flour or you'll end up with a sticky mess.

———————

· 500g grated daikon
· 225g rice flour
· 1 tsp caster sugar
· 1 tsp sea salt
· ½ tsp dried chilli flakes
· 2.5cm piece of ginger, peeled and finely grated
· 3 spring onions, trimmed and finely chopped
· 300ml cold water
· 2 tsp toasted sesame oil, plus an extra tsp for frying
· 2 tbsp rapeseed oil, for pan-frying

FOR THE FRIED GARLIC AND CHILLI OIL
· 150ml rapeseed oil
· 20–30 garlic cloves, very finely chopped
· Thumb of ginger, peeled and finely grated
· 2 tbsp red-skinned peanuts
· 5 dried red chillies, soaked in hot water for 30 minutes then drained and finely chopped
· 1 tsp Sichuan peppercorns, toasted and coarsely ground
· ¼ tsp black peppercorns, toasted and coarsely ground
· 2 spring onions, thickly sliced on the diagonal (including green parts)
· 1 tbsp Shaoxing wine
· 2 tbsp light soy sauce
· 1 tsp caster sugar

To make the daikon cake, place the grated daikon into a steamer and steam for 30 minutes over low heat until it is soft and translucent. I use a large bamboo steamer – you can find these online or at Asian supermarkets, they are inexpensive and a great investment. Set aside to cool.

In a large bowl, mix the rice flour, sugar, salt, chilli flakes, ginger and spring onions. Pour in the cold water mixed with the sesame oil and mix well, then fold in the cooled daikon. Grease a 2lb loaf tin then pour the mixture into it and steam over medium heat for 35–40 minutes or until a skewer inserted into the middle comes out clean. Stand to cool, then refrigerate for 6 hours or preferably overnight so it sets.

Turn the set daikon cake out of the tin onto a board and cut into half and then slice each half into 1cm-thick slices. You should get around 20 pieces.

Heat the 2 tablespoons of oil in a deep frying pan over medium heat and add a teaspoon of sesame oil. Once hot, fry the daikon cake slices

↓

a few at a time, for 2–3 minutes per batch, till dark golden on both sides. Lay on a platter and keep warm.

For the fried garlic and chilli oil, clean out the frying pan and pour in the rapeseed oil. Heat the oil in a wok over low-medium heat. Add the garlic and stir continuously for 2–3 minutes until just turning light golden then carefully drain through a fine heatproof sieve set over a heatproof bowl. Drain the garlic on kitchen paper.

Put the garlic oil back in the pan over medium heat, add the ginger and peanuts and stir-fry for 2–3 minutes until both are golden and fragrant. Add the chillies and peppercorns and fry briefly. Add the spring onions and half the fried garlic and fry for 20 seconds tossing with a spatula continuously. Finally, add the Shaoxing wine, soy sauce and sugar and heat till bubbling.

Spoon this over the daikon cake then top with the reserved fried garlic and serve immediately.

ROASTED CELERIAC STEAKS *with* KIMCHI BUTTER *and* KIMCHI, APPLE *and* PEAR SALSA

Celeriac may look brutish but it offers so much sweet, comforting promise beneath that strange exterior. Slow-cooking it like this and then pan-frying it with kimchi butter and topping it with kimchi, apple and pear salsa gives it a beautifying makeover.

———

Preheat the oven to 180°C/Fan 160°C/Gas Mark 4. Pierce the celeriac all over with a fork then rub all over with olive oil and season generously with salt. Wrap tightly in foil and roast for about 2 hours until your celeriac is meltingly tender.

In the meantime, make the kimchi, apple and pear salsa by simply mixing together all the ingredients.

Let the celeriac cool slightly then cut it into thick steaks (skin on). Heat a drizzle of oil in a pan over medium heat then add the celeriac and cook on both sides for 3–4 minutes each side till dark and caramelised, then add the kimchi butter and let it foam and bubble and baste the celeriac with it. Place on plates, spoon over the kimchi butter, top with the kimchi salsa and sesame seeds and serve.

· 1kg celeriac roots, scrubbed and cleaned
· 100g Kimchi Butter (page 229)
· Drizzle of rapeseed oil, for roasting and frying
· Sea salt
· Black or white sesame seeds, to garnish

FOR THE KIMCHI, APPLE AND PEAR SALSA

· 150g kimchi, very finely chopped
· 2 spring onions, thinly sliced (including green parts)
· 1 small sharp apple (i.e., Granny Smith), peeled, cored and finely diced
· 1 nashi pear, peeled, cored and finely diced
· 1 baby cucumber, seeded and finely diced
· 2 tbsp finely chopped coriander
· 2 tsp toasted sesame oil
· 1 tsp rice vinegar
· ½ tsp caster sugar
· Juice of 1 lime

ROASTED MUSCAT GRAPES
and FIGS *with* BURRATA
and BITTER LEAVES

Succulent clusters of grapes are baked to bursting, sticky yielding figs are pulled apart, and bejewelled pomegranates parade their beauty over bitter leaves and creamy burrata. This platter of good things is an ode to autumn – the season of mellow fruitfulness – and it tastes every bit as good as it looks.

———

Preheat the oven to 180°C/Fan 160°C/Gas Mark 4.

Cut the vines of the grapes with scissors, making sure you still leave them in fairly large bunches. Place them in a roasting tray. In a bowl, whisk together the pomegranate molasses, balsamic vinegar and oil. Season with salt and pepper then drizzle half over the grapes, tossing gently to make sure they are well coated. Scatter over the pink peppercorns and thyme. Roast in the oven for 5 minutes, turning the grapes halfway through, until the grapes are starting to burst and split. Set aside to cool to slightly.

In the meantime, arrange the chicory leaves over a serving platter then lay over the warm grapes, figs and torn burrata. Scrape the juices from the roasting tray into the remaining dressing and mix, then drizzle over the salad. Scatter over the walnuts and pomegranate seeds and serve.

· 500g Muscat grapes
· 1½ tbsp pomegranate molasses
· 1 tbsp balsamic vinegar
· 60ml extra virgin olive oil
· 1 tsp toasted pink peppercorns, coarsely ground
· A few sprigs of thyme
· 100g red chicory leaves
· 100g white chicory leaves
· 6 figs, torn or cut into quarters
· 3 balls of burrata
· 100g walnuts, roughly broken up
· Seeds from 1 small pomegranate
· Sea salt and black pepper

9
CONDIMENTS, CHUTNEYS AND PICKLES

CRAZY FOR CONDIMENTS

I've never been a collector of anything – not even as a child – but when we moved in together, my husband pointed out that my kitchen is a shrine to condiments. There are sticky jars and bottles of achaars, chilli sauces and ketchups stacked up precariously in my fridge door. I have many more than necessary, but I can't help but hoard. An excavation of my pantry reveals stacks of mustards, molasses, vinegars and oils. There are even some favourite condiments I buy in bulk because I have a fear of running out!

In delis, jams, chutneys and pickles hook me like bait. Even if my cupboards at home are full to bursting, I am insatiable. I greedily eye up what's new and fill up my shopping cart. On my travels abroad too, I seek out the local food markets so I can broaden my collection. It's a compulsion, a habit I just can't kick. I don't want to miss out on a single zing, umami hit, salty funk or spicy jolt. If I can dollop it, squeeze it, drizzle it or sprinkle it – I covet it.

My addiction began as a child when my mother caved in to allowing me to dot ketchup on my dinner as a means of coaxing me to clear my plate. I fell hard for its silky, vermillion, sweet-sour spike from first bite. I deployed it on rice, samosas, cheese on toast, potatoes – it was a thrilling little fix. As my taste buds matured, I graduated to chilli sauces and achaar. Mum would often make khitchadi – stewed lentils and rice which while nourishing can be lacklustre – and a little dab of her homemade sweet lime pickle became my weapon of choice against the war on blandness.

Over the years I have gained much joy from making my own condiments and pickles too. The glow of a row of jewel-coloured jars gleaming from my kitchen shelves gives me a Women's Institute-style sense of achievement but also adds critical pizazz to sagging or simple meals. I make dipping sauces, ketchups and most of all achaars – they are shortcuts to flavour I can use in marinades and sauces or just dribbled over eggs.

In September, as summer slides into autumn, it is a bountiful and beautiful fruit and vegetable moment that brings a languid feast of plumpness – weighty aubergines, fat courgettes and buxom tomatoes, peppers and stone fruits. The magic of vinegar, salt, sugar and oil infused with spices transforms my ripe glut into something that is so charismatic it virtually does jazz hands! This sunshine-infused harvest will see me through the winter dearth when there are slimmer pickings.

This chapter is dedicated to the unsung heroes of the kitchen that will delight and tantalise your taste buds that little bit more – things that can add complexity with a simple spoonful. There are compound butters and sauces that bolster and expand flavours, seasonings that make your meals multisensory, and piquant pickles that bring critical lightness and brightness to your meal. Many of these can also be happily eaten straight from the jar in the light of the fridge.

Next page (from left to right): Shaamba Pickles, Carrot and Jalapeno Achaar, Date and Tamarind Chutney, Goan Aubergine Pickle, Furukake, Chilli and Black Vinegar Dipping Sauce, Avocado and Coconut Chutney, Christmas Mango Chutney, Flavoured Butters

SHAAMBA PICKLES

Pickling vegetables and fruits is a tradition shared by many cultures. It's both sensible and delicious. This pickle mix infused with spices, garlic and tarragon is my favourite. A small bowl makes a great healthy snack or is perfect for waking up your taste buds before a meal.

———————

Begin by sterilising your jar by washing it well in warm soapy water. Place the jar in a large saucepan and cover with water. Bring to the boil and simmer for 10 minutes. Carefully drain the water from your jar. Transfer the jar and lid to a baking tray lined with a clean tea towel. Cover with a sheet of foil and place in a low oven until dry. Use straight from the oven.

Place all the prepared vegetables into the jar along with the lemon, chilli, garlic cloves, spices and tarragon. Bring the water to the boil then take it off the heat and add the salt, vinegar and lemon juice and stir to dissolve the salt. It should taste nice and salty with a lovely acidic punch. Pour into the jar, making sure the vegetables are submerged. Let the mixture cool, seal, and refrigerate for a minimum of 24 hours before eating. It will be good to eat for about 3 weeks, but it never seems to last that long.

- 3 Persian cucumbers, cut into 2cm-thick slices
- Bunch of radishes, trimmed and halved
- 2 candy beetroots, thinly sliced
- 2 golden beetroots, thinly sliced
- 2 turnips, peeled and cut into bite-sized chunks
- 2 nashi pears, cut into wedges
- 1 small cauliflower, broken into small florets
- 1 lemon, thinly sliced
- 1 long red chilli, split lengthways
- 4 garlic cloves, bruised
- 1 tbsp yellow mustard seeds
- 1 cinnamon stick
- A few sprigs of tarragon
- 1.2 litres water
- 2 tbsp coarse rock salt
- 375ml white wine vinegar
- 75ml lemon juice

CARROT *and* JALAPENO ACHAAR

222

In most Indian households, no meal is complete without a smidgen of achaar. Traditionally they are a sideshow to curries and dhals, but when you have a good one it will overshadow every player on the plate. This one brings a new lease of life to even the most sad and wilting carrots – a great way to use them so you don't lose them. Feel free to use regular orange carrots, but I love the colour contrast of the yellow and orange together.

———

Sprinkle the salt over the carrots in a colander, toss and leave for 30 minutes and then squeeze in a clean tea towel to get rid of the excess moisture.

Heat the oil in a wok over high heat. When hot, add the urid dhal and paanch phoron. As soon as they pop, add the asafoetida and curry leaves followed by the ginger and garlic and stir-fry till golden brown. Add the chilli powder, turmeric and jaggery. Once the jaggery has melted, take the pan off the heat, pour in the vinegar and stir. Mix in the carrots and chillies, stir well and store in a sterilised jar (see page 220 for sterilising method). Leave for 24 hours and then it's ready to eat. Store in the fridge. This pickle will keep well for up to 3 weeks.

· 1 tbsp sea salt
· 3 yellow carrots, cut into batons
· 3 orange carrots, cut into batons
· 60ml rapeseed oil
· 1 heaped tbsp skinned urid dhal
· 1 heaped tbsp paanch phoron
· Pinch of asafoetida
· 15 fresh curry leaves
· Thumb of ginger, peeled and thinly sliced
· 3 garlic cloves, finely chopped
· 1 tsp red chilli powder
· 1 tbsp ground turmeric
· 4 tbsp grated jaggery
· 5 tbsp white wine vinegar
· 3 green jalapeno chillies, split lengthways

GOAN AUBERGINE PICKLE

This is less of a condiment and more of a side dish. I love to eat it with a paratha and some yoghurt, as a side to dhal and rice, or grilled in a Breville toasted sandwich with cheese. It's sweet, sour and spicy – everything you want from a condiment.

————

Heat the oil in a wide frying pan over high heat. Scatter in the cumin, fenugreek, cinnamon, chilli flakes and fennel seeds and let the seeds crackle. Follow with the curry leaves, making sure the spices do not burn. Turn down the heat a little, add the garlic and ginger and fry until golden and fragrant. Drop in the chillies and let them cook till they lighten in colour. Sprinkle in the turmeric. Add the vinegar, sugar and salt and let it come to the boil, then stir in the aubergine chunks. Reduce the heat, cover and simmer over low heat for 30 minutes, stirring occasionally, until the oil floats to the top and the aubergine is tender. Cool and decant into a sterilised jar (see page 220 for sterilising method). The pickle will keep well in the fridge for up to 3 weeks.

- 2 tbsp rapeseed oil
- 2 tsp cumin seeds
- 1 tsp fenugreek seeds
- 1 cinnamon stick, broken up
- 1 tsp dried chilli flakes
- 2 tsp fennel seeds
- 1 stem fresh curry leaves
- 6 garlic cloves, thinly sliced
- 5cm piece of ginger, peeled and julienned
- 3 green finger chillies, slit lengthways
- 1 tsp ground turmeric
- 150ml white wine vinegar
- 75g light soft brown sugar
- Sea salt, to taste
- 2 large aubergines (1kg), cut into 2cm chunks

CHRISTMAS MANGO CHUTNEY

224

Mangoes are full of sweet promise. This sweet and sultry chutney brings a taste of the tropical to our Christmas cheeseboard every year. It also makes a great dip or marinade mixed with yoghurt – try it poured over chunks of paneer or halloumi before roasting for a moreish starter.

————

- · 1 tbsp rapeseed oil
- · 1 small red onion, finely chopped
- · 2 garlic cloves, finely chopped
- · 1 tbsp peeled and finely grated ginger
- · 1 tsp ground allspice
- · ½ tsp dried chilli flakes
- · 1 tbsp hot madras curry powder
- · 2 large medium-ripe mangoes, peeled, pitted and diced
- · 100g light muscovado sugar
- · 60ml apple cider vinegar
- · 50g golden raisins
- · Finely grated zest and juice of 1 lime

Heat the oil in a frying pan over low heat, add the onion and fry for 15 minutes until caramelised, then add the garlic and ginger and sauté until fragrant. Now add the allspice, chilli flakes and madras curry powder and fry briefly, then stir in the mango, muscovado sugar, vinegar and raisins. Bring the mixture to the boil then reduce the heat and cook, stirring occasionally, until it begins to thicken. Cook for 15 minutes then remove from the heat and transfer the chutney to a heatproof bowl. Stir in the lime zest and juice. Cool before serving. The chutney will keep in the fridge for up to 3 weeks.

GREEN CORIANDER *and* MINT CHUTNEY

Along with date and tamarind chutney (see page 226), this is one of the two most essential chutneys in an Indian kitchen. It is great for bringing a verdant freshness to fried things like samosas and bhajis although I also love a thin spread of this in a cheese sandwich.

————

- · 100g fresh coriander, including stalks
- · 25g fresh mint leaves, picked
- · 2 tbsp unsalted skinned peanuts, soaked in hot water for 30 minutes then drained
- · 1–2 green chillies
- · Juice of 1 lime
- · 1 tsp caster sugar
- · Chaat masala, to taste
- · Sea salt, to taste
- · 75ml ice-cold water

Simply place all the ingredients in a food processor with half the ice-cold water and blend to a fine, smooth paste, then add the remaining water and blend again. Put in a bowl or a jar and store in the refrigerator for up to 3 days.

Makes about 250g

AVOCADO *and* COCONUT CHUTNEY

Think of this like an Indian guacamole. It is great with the avocado aloo chaat (see page 48) but equally lovely with a handful of corn chips or spread on toast. Use creamy Hass avocados for best results and plenty of zingy lime juice to cut through their voluptuous fattiness.

———

Blitz the coconut in a blender along with 2 tablespoons of water till you have a paste. Next, add the ginger, garlic and chillies and blend again, then scoop the flesh from the avocados, add it to the blender and blend to a smooth puree. Heat the oil in a frying pan over high heat and, once it's hot, add the mustard seeds. As soon as they pop, sprinkle in the asafoetida, curry leaves and chillies till they crackle then pour them over the avocado puree and stir. Season to taste and add lime juice – it should be lovely and zingy. The chutney will keep in the fridge for up to 3 days.

- 50g fresh or frozen grated coconut, defrosted
- Thumb of ginger, peeled and roughly chopped
- 1 garlic clove, roughly chopped
- 1–2 green finger chillies
- 2 large avocados
- 2 tbsp rapeseed oil
- 1 tsp brown mustard seeds
- Pinch of asafoetida
- 12 fresh curry leaves
- 2 dried red Kashmiri chillies, broken up
- Sea salt
- Juice of 1 juicy lime

Makes about 150ml

CHILLI *and* BLACK VINEGAR DIPPING SAUCE

I love Chinese black vinegar – it has a sweet, well balanced, fruity and nuanced flavour rather than just being a harsh acid bomb. The addition of it to this dipping sauce makes it perfect for deep-fried foods like spring rolls or rich steamed dumplings.

———

This couldn't be simpler – whisk together all the ingredients and voila!

- 80ml Chinkiang vinegar
- 60ml light soy sauce
- 1 long red chilli, finely chopped
- 1 tbsp peeled and finely grated ginger
- 1 tbsp finely chopped coriander
- 2 tsp sesame oil
- 1 tsp caster sugar

DATE *and* TAMARIND CHUTNEY

226

Sweet, sour, tart and spicy – this chutney is an essential ingredient for nearly all chaats, but will spruce up and bring joy to many other dishes. I love to add a spoonful or so to the base of a potato curry to add complexity or simply eat it drizzled over roasted sweet potatoes. It is addictive stuff!

———

· 10 pitted dates
· 5 tbsp tamarind concentrate
· 1 tbsp palm sugar, grated jaggery or soft brown sugar
· Red chilli powder, to taste
· 1 tsp toasted cumin seeds, crushed
· ¼ tsp ground cinnamon
· 1 tsp chaat masala
· Black salt (kala namak), to taste – optional

Put the dates in a saucepan and cover with a little water. When it has come to the boil, reduce the heat and simmer for 10 minutes until the dates are very soft. Stir in the tamarind concentrate and then puree with a stick blender or in a food processor. Strain into a bowl through a fine metal sieve to remove any residue. Mix in the remaining ingredients and stir in a little water if it is too thick – it should have the consistency of a ketchup. Refrigerate and cool. The chutney will keep for about 3 weeks in a sterilised jar (see page 220 for sterilising method).

FURUKAKE

Furukake goes way beyond salt and pepper – it delivers umami. It often contains bonito which I have replaced with salty crisp-fried shallots instead. I love this sprinkled over noodles, ramen bowls or even just simple boiled eggs at breakfast.

———

· 6 sheets nori
· 6 tbsp white sesame seeds, toasted
· 3 tbsp black sesame seeds
· 3 tsp crisp-fried shallots
· 2 tsp sea salt
· 2½ tsp caster sugar

Toast the nori sheets over an open flame if you have a gas hob, or dry fry on a hot pan till it crisps up. This should only take a few seconds. Crumble into tiny pieces – you can use a pestle and mortar or a spice grinder if you like. Mix with the sesame seeds, crisp-fried shallots, salt and sugar and set aside. Put it in an airtight container and it will keep for 1 month.

QUICK
PICKLED INDIAN ONIONS

There was always a special place on the table and in my father's heart
for these pickled onions. Our dinner table was rarely complete without
a bowl of them. I like to pile these into a grilled cheese sandwich, on
a fatty avocado toast or toss them through a salad. They especially
bring a lightness and brightness to dhals and curries. They're easy to
make and great to have at hand.

———————

Heat the vinegar, sugar and salt in a saucepan with the peppercorns
and cinnamon stick or cassia bark. Bring to a simmer and allow
the salt and sugar to dissolve, then take off the heat and stir in the
chaat masala.

Place the onions in a large sieve and pour over water from a freshly
boiled kettle, then refresh in ice-cold water and drain well. Pack the
onion and the green chillies into a 500g sterilised jar (see page 220 for
sterilising method) then pour over the brine and seal. Cool then chill –
your pickles will be ready to eat in 1 hour. Consume within 2 weeks.

· 300ml white wine vinegar
· 3 tbsp caster sugar
· 1 tbsp sea salt
· A few black peppercorns
· 1 small cinnamon stick or piece
  of cassia bark
· 1 heaped tsp chaat masala
· 3 red onions, very thinly sliced
  into rings
· 1–2 green chillies, slit lengthways

FLAVOURED BUTTERS

228

Flavoured or compound butters offer an instant opportunity to add some sass and flavour to a dish. They are great melted over roasted vegetables (I love the lime pickle butter on carrots and parsnips) or to run through pasta or finish off a soup or a dhal (preserved lemon, mint and pul biber butter). Put them on toast, a crumpet, a baked potato or melted over the nubs of a corn on the cob and you'll have an instant flavour upgrade.

———————

Stir all the ingredients together in a bowl until well combined.

Lay out a long sheet of cling film on a worktop and smooth out any creases by wiping with a damp cloth.

Spoon the butter out onto the centre of the cling film and form into a neat 15cm log. Tightly wrap it up and roll until smooth and secure with a knot at each end.

Store the compound butter in the freezer. When ready to use, remove from the freezer for 10 minutes or so, slice off the amount of butter you require, then return the log to the freezer for another time.

KIMCHI BUTTER
· 225g unsalted butter, softened
· 150g kimchi, pureed
· 1 tbsp gochujang

LIME PICKLE BUTTER
· 225g unsalted butter, softened
· 3 heaped tbsp lime pickle
· 5 tbsp finely chopped coriander
· 3 tbsp lime juice

FERMENTED CHILLI BEAN PASTE BUTTER
· 225g unsalted butter, softened
· 2 heaped tbsp fermented chilli bean paste
· Thumb of ginger, peeled and finely grated

PRESERVED LEMON, MINT AND PUL BIBER BUTTER
· 225g unsalted butter, softened
· Rind of 4 preserved lemons, pureed
· 4 heaped tbsp dried mint
· 4 heaped tbsp Turkish pepper flakes (pul biber)

NORI MISO BUTTER
· 225g unsalted butter, softened
· 50g shiro miso
· Thumb of ginger, peeled and finely grated
· 6 toasted nori sheets, blended in a food processor
  till finely chopped
· 3 heaped tbsp toasted white sesame seeds

SPICED HONEY AND SAFFRON BUTTER
· 225g unsalted butter, softened
· 2 tsp ground ginger
· 2 tsp ground cinnamon
· 2 tsp ground allspice
· 1 tsp ground turmeric
· Generous grating of nutmeg
· 1 heaped tsp saffron strands
· 4 tbsp honey
· 8 fat garlic cloves, pureed

DATE AND ORANGE BLOSSOM BUTTER
· 225g unsalted butter, softened
· 125g soft pitted dates, pureed
· 2 fat pinches of salt
· 1 tbsp orange blossom water

10
CAKES, DESSERTS AND PUDDINGS

OBJECT OF MY CONFECTION

I was 13 when I first visited Paris. I stepped into a bakery in the First Arrondissement and was immediately seduced. It was a baroque, rosy-marbled bordello of patisserie. The air was perfumed with yeast and caramel, pheromones and grown-up dark chocolate. The polished glass counter displayed row upon row of confections to ogle – miniature sugary pin-ups; there were dark glossy domes whose plush secret interiors revealed airy raspberry mousse and framboise-soaked sponge, strawberry tartlets glistening lasciviously with sticky glaze, overstuffed cream horns that throbbed with vanilla and neat stacks of macarons the colour of love-flushed cheeks.

When people banter that eating dessert is better than having sex, they may in fact not be joking. Eating sweet things gives you a surge in dopamine and serotonin, just as a giddy sexual encounter would. They make you feel euphoric, enraptured and energised. It's impossible not to fall hard for the golden burnish of caramel, the titillating jiggle of panna cotta, the coquettish bosoms of meringue or the generous swell of soufflé. You are not the only fool to look for love in mounds of just-whipped cream or to be taken in by the promise of a still-warm chocolate cake. Puddings caress you with ethereal textures and flavours. In patisseries, their sensual formation encourages a sort of gratifying lingering. You may find yourself swept away, helpless, drawn in by their magnetic pull that ends as soon as the last spoonful is eaten.

When I first met my husband, we both played a stimulating game of seduction – a vigorous campaign to win and to woo each other. He flattered me with a charm offensive that included several romantic gestures. He organised carousel dates that took us to romantic spots in the city and beyond, moonlit walks and engaging telephone conversations that started in the early evening and ended just as the light of the rising sun was flooding my bedroom. I, in return, dabbed on whispers of expensive perfume he had to lean in close to sniff. I wore dresses that encouraged him to stare and put on a grand show thick with ambiguity, process, tension and playfulness that left him quite bewildered. Yet somehow my opponent stood undefeated, until one serendipitous afternoon, when quite unexpectedly I located his Achilles heel.

I'd been testing dessert recipes. My kitchen was chaotic but there on the worktop, laid out like bait, was a beauty pageant of pretty confections – a meringue roulade bursting with foraged blackberries and cream, a frothy trifle with a wibbling jelly built on faith and a whisper of gelatin, a soufflé with a marshmallow heart and a checkerboard of varying sponges, cakes and éclairs. He picked up the soufflé and handled it as delicately as if it were a piece of rare, lost art. He raised it to the level of his chest and bent over to meet it with his nose to savour its scent. He dug a fork into its interior, and as his lips met the tines of the fork, he gasped. He seemed to be eating it in rapturous slow motion. Sated, he fell onto the sofa, and fell for me.

In our pleasure-abstinent modern lives focused on work, speed and capitalism, desserts encourage you to slow down and relish in the art of creativity and self-gratification. To make them for yourself is free-spirited, luxurious and defiant. They are also an important tool to show love or at least to persuade others to your point of view! Stop and smell the vanilla before life passes you by.

ILES FLOTTANT *with* SAFFRON *and* CARDAMOM CUSTARD *and* PISTACHIO CARAMEL

The name of this French dessert translates to 'floating island'. It refers to silky clouds of soft meringue islands floating on a sea of pourable custard that I certainly wouldn't mind being a castaway on. I flavour the custard with fragrant cardamom and an intoxicating pinch of saffron. The praline brings a welcome crunch to the ethereal fluffiness of it all.

———————

First make the praline. Heat the sugar and water in a saucepan over medium-high heat until the sugar dissolves, then brush down the sides of the pan with a wet pastry brush and bring to the boil, swirling the pan as the mixture starts to caramelise, until you have a dark caramel. Remove from heat, stir in the pistachios and salt with a lightly oiled fork, tip onto a lightly oiled baking tray and leave to set for about 30 minutes before coarsely crushing with a pestle and mortar.

To make the custard, combine the milk, cream, saffron and cardamom in a heavy-based saucepan and bring to a simmer. Whisk the egg yolks and sugar in a bowl until pale and creamy, pour over half the cream mixture and whisk to combine. Pour the egg mixture back into the pan and stir with remaining cream mixture. Return the pan to medium heat and cook, stirring continuously, until the mixture coats the back of a spoon. Strain and refrigerate.

To make the meringue, whisk the egg whites with the salt in the clean bowl of a stand mixer fitted with the whisk attachment until they form soft peaks, then gradually add the sugar, a little at a time, until you have smooth and glossy stiff peaks.

Simmer the milk and water in a wide pan over low-medium heat. Using 2 tablespoons dipped in hot water, scoop quenelles of meringue and poach in batches for about 2 minutes on each side until just firm. Transfer with a slotted spoon to kitchen paper.

Divide the cold custard into 6 dishes and place meringues on top. Finish with praline and flaked almonds, and gold leaf if showing off!

FOR THE PISTACHIO PRALINE
· 100g caster sugar
· 25ml water
· 100g pistachios
· Pinch of salt

FOR THE CUSTARD
· 250ml whole milk
· 250ml double cream
· Pinch of saffron threads
· Seeds from 4 green cardamom pods, crushed
· 5 egg yolks
· 100g caster sugar

FOR THE MERINGUE
· 4 eggs whites
· Pinch of salt
· 50g golden caster sugar
· 1 litre whole milk
· 500ml water

TO GARNISH
· Handful of toasted flaked almonds
· Gold leaf – optional

MANGO-MISU

This dessert takes the main elements of a classic tiramisu – mascarpone, boozy zabaione and sponge fingers – but swaps out the coffee for sweet mangoes instead. It is rich, creamy, lethally delicious yet still light as a feather. It is all the sweet rapture of summer in a bowl.

Make the Thai basil sugar by blitzing together all the ingredients in a food processor until you have a vibrantly green coarse sugar. Set aside until required.

To make the mango syrup, mix together the mango juice, rum and lime juice and heat gently in a small saucepan over low heat until it comes to a simmer then set aside.

To make the zabaione, whisk the egg yolks, sugar, rum and 1 tablespoon of water in a heatproof bowl over a saucepan of simmering water until pale and thick (making sure the water doesn't touch the bowl), then set aside to cool. Whisk the mascarpone, crème fraîche and lime zest together to combine, then fold through the zabaione. Whisk the egg whites in a separate bowl till soft peaks form, then fold them through the mascarpone mixture.

To assemble, briefly dip half the savoiardi in the syrup and arrange in a 25cm serving dish. Spoon over half the mascarpone mixture over and then layer over half the sliced mangoes and half the passion fruit pulp. Follow with the remaining savoiardi dipped in syrup, the mangoes and passion fruit pulp and finally dollop over the remaining mascarpone mixture and smooth the surface. Refrigerate for 4–6 hours.

When ready to serve, sprinkle the Thai basil sugar over the surface.

· 500g mascarpone cheese
· 250g crème fraîche
· Zest of 2 limes
· 2 egg whites
· 1 × 200g packet savoiardi biscuits or sponge fingers
· 6 ripe mangoes such as alphonso or kesar, peeled and sliced
· Pulp from 6 passion fruits

FOR THE THAI BASIL SUGAR
· 30g unsweetened desiccated coconut, toasted
· Zest of 2 limes
· Bunch of Thai basil leaves
· 100g caster sugar

FOR THE MANGO SYRUP
· 125ml mango juice
· 40ml rum
· Juice of 1 lime

FOR THE ZABAIONE
· 2 egg yolks
· 50g caster sugar
· 25ml rum

SPICED APPLE *and* BLACKBERRY MERINGUE ROULADE

Even living in the city, we are never far from a blackberry bush. In autumn, the brambles are heavy with them – free garnet jewels ripe for the picking, providing endless opportunities to make preserves or a pudding or just eating as they are. I am always stunned by their gutsiness, by their ferocity that tastes of somewhere remote and otherworldly, and their sheer, sour voltage. Pairing them with apples and sweet baked meringue is one of my favourite ways to eat them.

————

To make the spiced fruit filling, put all the ingredients, except the blackberries, in a saucepan set over medium heat. Heat the liquid until just boiling, then reduce the heat to the lowest temperature and poach until the apples are just tender, but still have bite. Take off the heat, cool for 30 minutes, then add the blackberries, leaving them to infuse in the poaching liquid. Once completely cool, drain. Reserve the liquid as a mixer for cocktails.

To make the meringue, begin by mixing the blackberries, 25g of the caster sugar and the water in a small pan. Bring to the boil and simmer for 5 minutes until the berries are very soft. Blend until smooth and strain through a sieve into a bowl, discarding the seeds and then cool.

Preheat the oven to 200°C/Fan 180°C/Gas Mark 6. Line a 23 × 33cm baking tray with parchment paper and lightly grease with oil.

In the bowl of a stand mixer fitted with the whisk attachment, whisk the egg whites until stiff. Gradually whisk in the rest of the caster sugar, a little at a time, and continue whisking until thick and glossy. Fold in the vanilla extract, vinegar and cornflour. Spread the meringue evenly into the prepared baking tray. Dollop tablespoons of blackberry purée over the meringue and use a knife or skewer to swirl it through the meringue. Bake for 10 minutes, then reduce the temperature to 160°C/Fan 140°C/Gas Mark 3 and cook for a further 10 minutes.

FOR THE SPICED APPLE AND BLACKBERRIES
- 1 Granny Smith and 1 Bramley apple, cored, peeled and cut into 2cm chunks
- 1 star anise
- 1 cinnamon stick
- ¼ tsp black peppercorns
- 1 vanilla pod, split
- 1 strip of orange rind
- 300ml marsala wine
- 200g blackberries

FOR THE MERINGUE
- 50g blackberries
- 225g caster sugar
- 30ml water
- 4 egg whites
- 1 tsp vanilla extract
- 1 tsp white vinegar
- 2 tsp cornflour, sifted
- Icing sugar, for dusting

FOR THE FILLING
- 150ml double cream
- 1 tbsp icing sugar
- 1 vanilla pod, seeds scraped
- 150g mascarpone, beaten to loosen

Dust another sheet of parchment paper with icing sugar.

Remove the meringue from the oven and leave to cool for 2–3 minutes on the tray, before turning it out onto the second piece of parchment paper. Cool for a further 5 minutes, then gently peel off the first sheet of parchment paper from the top of the meringue. Roll up the meringue from the long side until ready to use.

To make the filling, whip the double cream with the icing sugar and vanilla seeds in a bowl then fold in the beaten mascarpone.

Unroll the meringue, spread the cream mix over the surface, top with the drained poached fruit – discarding the whole spices and orange rind – and roll up again as tightly as you can, using the paper to help you. Refrigerate for at least 1 hour to firm up, then serve in slices.

STRAWBERRY FALOODA MILK CAKE

British colonial rule may have divided up India, Pakistan and Bangladesh, but we are all united in our love of falooda – a rose-tinted milkshake textured with bubbly basil seeds and noodles. Faloodas come in many flavours, from mango to pistachio, but my favourite is what I consider the original and best – rooh afza – made with a thick concentrated floral syrup that turns milk Barbie pink. Rooh afza, which translates enigmatically to 'soul refresher' is easily found in Indian and Pakistani supermarkets. Here, inspired by my friend Ravneet Gill's excellent Rasmalai Cake, I have used rooh afza-flavoured milk to make a sort of tres leches cake. If you can't find basil seeds, use chia seeds which have a similar tapioca-like texture when hydrated.

———

- 225g plain flour
- 1 tsp baking powder
- ½ tsp salt
- 5 eggs
- 175g caster sugar
- 1 tsp rosewater
- 115g unsalted butter, melted, plus extra for greasing

FOR THE FALOODA MILK
- 50ml rooh afza
- 200g condensed milk
- 250ml whole milk
- 300ml double cream

FOR THE TOPPING
- 300g strawberries, sliced
- 2 tbsp basil seeds
- 1 tbsp rosewater
- 1 tsp caster sugar
- 300ml double cream
- Dried rose petals, for sprinkling
- Crushed pistachios, for sprinkling

Preheat the oven to 180°C/Fan 160°C/Gas Mark 4 and lightly grease a 3-litre (33 × 23cm) baking dish with butter.

In a jug or bowl, whisk together all the ingredients for the falooda milk and leave in the fridge to chill till required.

Sift the flour, baking powder and salt into a bowl. Put the eggs and sugar in the bowl of a stand mixer fitted with the whisk attachment and whisk on high speed for about 7 minutes until thick and pale (or whisk in a bowl with a hand-held electric whisk). Fold in the flour mixture and rosewater, then fold in the melted butter. Spoon into the baking dish, smooth the top and bake for 30–35 minutes until golden brown, and a skewer inserted into the cake comes out clean.

When you remove the cake from the oven, prick it all over with a skewer and keep warm. Pour over the falooda milk and leave to cool to room temperature. Cover and refrigerate overnight.

To serve, mix together the strawberries, basil seeds, rosewater and sugar and set aside. Before serving, gently whisk the double cream in a bowl until it has a soft, rumpled bedsheet texture. Spread the cream over the surface of the cake and then spoon the strawberries over the cake. Top with rose petals and crushed pistachios.

VEGAN PIÑA COLADA TRIFLE *with* TAPIOCA CUSTARD

Making desserts for those you love is like gifting them a piece of luxury – you've lavished such time and effort on something so fleeting, destined never to last very long. This trifle, based on the popular rum-based holiday cocktail, is a tribute to one of my favourite people in the world – my niece Avneet who is a dedicated vegan. Trifles are easy to adapt as long as there are frothy layers of fruit, sponge, cream and custard. This one packs a plant-based wallop of all of these and it's so creamy and indulgent that you'll barely believe there's no dairy in it.

————

Begin by making the cake. Preheat the oven to 160°C/Fan 140°C/Gas Mark 3. Oil and line the base and sides of a 20cm cake tin with greaseproof paper.

In the bowl of a stand mixer fitted with the paddle attachment, beat the margarine and sugar till light and fluffy. Sift in the plain flour, baking powder and bicarbonate of soda, then add the ground almonds, desiccated coconut and salt. Add the coconut milk, lime zest and juice and beat well until the ingredients are thoroughly combined and the mixture is smooth. Spoon the cake mix into the prepared tin, tap the tin gently on the work surface to level out the mixture and bake for 30 minutes. Put a skewer in the centre and if it comes out dry, the cake is ready. Sit the cake tin on a wire rack and leave to cool before removing the cake from the tin.

To make the jelly, measure the pineapple juice and reserved pineapple tin juice (it should be about 375ml) into a saucepan. Add the sugar and agar agar powder and whisk thoroughly till the sugar has dissolved. Heat over high heat until it reaches a simmer then reduce the temperature to low and continue to heat for 1 minute, stirring constantly. Add the lime zest and juice and take off the heat immediately. Pour into a 500ml volume shallow tray or container, add the pineapple chunks, cool and refrigerate for 30 minutes to set.

· White or dark rum, to taste
· ½ fresh pineapple, sliced into carpaccio-thin slices with a mandoline
· Coconut shavings, to garnish
· Zest of 2 limes
· A few sprigs of fresh pineapple mint or regular mint

FOR THE LIME AND COCONUT SPONGE
· 150g margarine
· 175g caster sugar
· 200g plain flour
· 2 tsp baking powder
· ½ tsp bicarbonate of soda
· 50g ground almonds
· 50g unsweetened desiccated coconut
· Pinch of salt
· 150ml unsweetened coconut drinking milk (not from tins)
· Zest and juice of 2 limes

FOR THE PINEAPPLE JELLY
· 1 litre unsweetened pineapple juice
· 2 × 435g tins pineapple chunks, drained and liquid reserved
· 50g caster sugar
· 2 tsp agar agar powder
· Zest and juice of 1 lime

To make the tapioca custard, wash the tapioca pearls thoroughly in cold water and then place in a saucepan and cover with enough boiling water to cover the pearls by 2cm. Simmer over low-medium heat for 15–20 minutes. Cooking times vary according to the size of the pearls, but once cooked they should be tender and translucent. Drain and rinse in cold water again.

In the meantime, measure the coconut milk into a saucepan and remove 2 tablespoons of it into a mixing bowl. Add the salt, sugar and pandan (if using) into the pan. Heat gently until the sugar has dissolved and it comes to a simmer.

Add the cornflour to the cold reserved coconut milk and stir to make a paste. Pour half the hot milk onto the paste, whisking as you do, then tip the mixture back into the pan. Place the pan back over low heat and stir until the custard has thickened – this should take 6–7 minutes. Bubble gently for 4–5 minutes then take off the heat and chill. Stir the tapioca into the custard and chill. Once cold, add more coconut milk, if required, to loosen.

To assemble, tear the sponge into rough chunks and place in the bottom of a 2.5-litre trifle dish. Sprinkle with rum to taste and then turn out the jelly – chop into pieces and place on top of the cake. Give the cooled custard a brief whisk, then pour it over the top of the jelly. Chill for 1–2 hours until the custard has set.

Whip all of the ingredients for the cream together in a bowl until you get soft peaks and spoon over the top of the set custard. Chill until ready to serve then decorate with pineapple slices, shaved coconut, lime zest and mint.

FOR THE TAPIOCA CUSTARD
· 120g small tapioca pearls
· 1.3 litres coconut milk
· Pinch of salt
· 100g caster sugar
· 1 pandan leaf, tied in a knot – optional
· 65g cornflour

FOR THE CREAM TOPPING
· 300ml whippable plant-based cream
· 75ml coconut cream
· 50ml dark or white rum
· 2 tsp icing sugar

RHUBARB *and* SICHUAN PEPPER CRUMBLE GALETTES

250

I adore rhubarb – celery dressed up in a hot-pink silk sari, feverishly scarlet in February when everything else is so muted and bleak. It stands out – it is elusive, complex and defiant – a vegetable masquerading as a fruit that refuses to be sweet or compliant. I have paired it here with Sichuan peppercorns which have a mildly citrus flavour and a pleasing tingling effect that is both delicious and surprising.

————

Preheat the oven to 180°C/Fan 160°C/Gas Mark 4.

Arrange the rhubarb snugly in a single layer in a baking dish, scatter over the sugar and orange rind, drizzle with the orange juice and sprinkle over the peppercorns. Cover tightly with foil and roast for 15 minutes until rhubarb is tender but still holding its shape. Cool in the syrup then remove from the syrup and set aside. Cook the syrup until it thickens. Set aside to cool.

Increase the oven temperature to 200°C/Fan 180°C/Gas Mark 6.

Cut six 10cm circles from the pastry, prick them all over with a fork and brush with the beaten egg. Chill in the fridge.

To make the crumble, whizz the biscuits in a blender to a coarse crumb then add the flour, butter and sugar and blend again till you have coarse crumbs. Fold through the almonds and peppercorns. Scatter it over the pastry rounds and bake for 15 minutes, or until the pastry is golden brown and crisp, turning the tray halfway. Cool on a wire rack.

To make the rhubarb ripple cream, roughly crush a third of the rhubarb with a fork. Whisk the double cream and icing sugar in a bowl with a whisk or hand-held electric whisk until it forms peaks and fold into the mascarpone. Swirl through the crushed rhubarb for a ripple effect.

Top the galettes with the cream – with a piping bag or a spoon – add slices of cooked rhubarb and drizzle over some rhubarb syrup. Serve.

· 1 × 320g sheet of ready-rolled all-butter puff pastry
· 1 egg, beaten

FOR THE RHUBARB
· 500g rhubarb, sliced into 8cm lengths
· 200g caster sugar
· Thin pared strips of rind and juice of 3 oranges
· 1 tsp Sichuan peppercorns, roughly cracked

FOR THE CRUMBLE
· 25g ginger biscuits
· 40g plain flour
· 30g butter
· 25g light brown sugar
· 30g flaked almonds
· ½ tsp cracked Sichuan peppercorns

FOR THE RHUBARB RIPPLE CREAM
· 200ml double cream
· 25g icing sugar
· 200g mascarpone cheese

ORANGE *and* FENNEL CAKE
with CANDIED FENNEL *and* ORANGES

While using fennel seeds is common in baking, I have used the whole bulb here much like you would use carrots in perennially popular carrot cake. It brings a sophisticated and grown-up aniseed note to the cake and pairs deliciously with oranges. The sliced candied bulb also makes for a graceful and unusual decoration.

———

**FOR THE CANDIED FENNEL
AND ORANGE**

· 1 small fennel bulb, cut into 4mm-
thick slices
· 1 orange, cut into 4mm-thick slices
· 175g caster sugar
· 175ml water

FOR THE CAKE BATTER

· 350g fennel, coarsely grated
(about 2 small bulbs)
· 350g caster sugar
· 250g spelt flour
· 200ml rapeseed oil
· 4 large eggs
· 60g cut mixed candied peel
· 75g walnuts, roughly chopped
· 1 tsp baking powder
· Zest of 1 orange
· Fat pinch of salt
· 3 tsp fennel seeds, toasted
and crushed
· 1 tsp ground ginger

**FOR THE FENNEL
AND ORANGE ICING**

· 340g cream cheese
· 150g icing sugar, sifted
· 2 tsp toasted fennel seeds,
finely crushed
· Finely grated zest of 2 small oranges
plus 2 tbsp orange juice

Begin by making the candied fennel and orange – you will need to dry out the fennel and orange slices for 6 hours or overnight. Put the fennel in a medium saucepan, cover with cold water and bring to the boil. Drain and set aside. Add the sugar and water to a large saucepan and bring to a simmer, stirring till the sugar has dissolved. Carefully add the fennel and orange slices and simmer very gently for 30–45 minutes till tender and translucent and the liquid is syrupy, turning them occasionally. Lift out the fennel and orange slices with a fork and lay over a wire rack placed over a baking sheet to dry out overnight.

Preheat the oven to 180°C/Fan 160°C/Gas Mark 4 and oil and line the base and sides of a 20cm square cake tin with baking paper. The cake mix couldn't be any easier: beat together the grated fennel, sugar, flour, oil, eggs, mixed peel, walnuts, baking powder, orange zest, salt and spices in the bowl of a stand mixer fitted with the paddle attachment on a low speed, then mix on medium speed for 2 minutes until everything is well combined. Pour the batter into the prepared tin and bake in the centre of the oven for 1 hour 15 minutes–1 hour 30 minutes, until the cake is golden brown and a skewer inserted into the centre comes out clean. Leave to cool in the tin for 20 minutes, then turn out onto a wire rack to cool completely. Once cool, halve the cake horizontally with a serrated knife.

To make the icing, whisk together all the ingredients in the bowl of the stand mixer fitted with the whisk attachment. Once smooth, spread half the icing on the cut side of the bottom half of the cake, and then sandwich on the top and spread the remaining cream over the top surface. Decorate with the candied fennel and orange.

STONE FRUIT *with* BURNT HONEY ICE CREAM *and* SWEET DUKKAH

254

Ice cream always brings the promise of happiness and fun. The ephemeral freshness of this homemade one sets it apart from anything that you can buy in the shops. Scorching the honey brings a subtle smokiness that is enhanced by plump charred summer stone fruits hidden in its creamy crevices. This is a dessert made for barbecues, summer entertaining and good times.

———————

First make the ice cream. Cook the honey in a heavy-based saucepan over medium heat for 5 minutes or until dark coloured, add 2 tablespoons of cold water to stop it burning and remove from the heat. Heat the milk and cream in a separate saucepan and bring to a simmer. Place the egg yolks and sugar in a bowl and whisk until thick and pale, then gradually whisk in the hot milk mixture, and then the burnt honey. Return the mixture to the heavy-based saucepan and stir over low heat for 7–8 minutes until the mixture thickens enough to coat the back of a wooden spoon, then add the orange blossom water. Do not boil. Remove from heat and strain through a fine sieve into a bowl and cool. Refrigerate and, once completely chilled, pour into an ice cream maker and churn until frozen.

For the sweet dukkah, preheat the oven to 180°C/Fan 160°C/ Gas Mark 4. In a bowl, mix together all the ingredients. Spread over a lined baking sheet and bake for 8–10 minutes until nutty and toasty. Cool then roughly bash in a pestle and mortar.

For the charred stone fruit, heat a griddle pan or a barbecue till hot. Brush the stone fruit with a little oil and cook, cut side down, for 2–3 minutes until caramelised. Turn and cook on the other side for 1–2 minutes more until tender but still holding their shape. Serve the warm fruit with scoops of ice cream and a scattering of pomegranate seeds and dukkah.

- 1kg stone fruit such as peaches, nectarines and apricots, cut into halves and wedges and cherries left whole (stones removed)
- 500g soft berries such as strawberries, raspberries
- Large handful of pomegranate seeds
- Drizzle of olive oil

FOR THE ICE CREAM
- 125g runny honey
- 500ml whole milk
- 250ml double cream
- 6 egg yolks
- 30g caster sugar
- 1 tbsp orange blossom water

FOR THE SWEET DUKKAH
- 40g pistachios
- 40g pine nuts
- 40g toasted almonds, roughly chopped
- 1 tbsp poppy seeds
- 2 tbsp white sesame seeds
- Zest of 1 large orange
- 1 heaped tsp ground cinnamon
- ¼ tsp ground cardamom
- 2 tbsp runny honey
- Fat pinch of sea salt

EASY UPSIDE-DOWN WHITE CHOCOLATE, RASPBERRY *and* PASSION FRUIT PUDDING

Constructed from a dome of soft spongy ready-made Swiss roll (see, I said it was easy!) filled with set custard, fragrant passion fruit and tart raspberries – this dessert fits somewhere between a summer pudding and a trifle. It's simple to make, yet looks like a showstopper and makes a wonderful centrepiece for a festive table. Set it overnight so the custard adequately soaks and seeps through the sponge. Serve with mounds of whipped cream.

———————

Line a 1.8-litre pudding bowl with cling film. Cut the Swiss rolls into 1cm-thick slices and line base and sides of the bowl with the slices. Drizzle with the rum and set aside, reserving the remaining jam roll slices.

To make the custard, put the milk, cream and vanilla seeds in a saucepan and bring to a simmer. Meanwhile, whisk the egg yolks and caster sugar in a bowl. Whisk in the warm milk mixture, then return to the pan and stir over medium heat until the custard reaches 85°C on a sugar thermometer or thickly coats the back of a spoon – this should take about 10 minutes. Meanwhile, soak the gelatine leaves in a bowl of cold water. Remove the custard from the heat, squeeze the water from the gelatine, add it to the custard and stir to dissolve, adding the white chocolate and letting it melt too. Let it cool slightly, then stir in the passion fruit pulp and the raspberries and pour into the jam roll-lined bowl. Top with the remaining Swiss roll slices, cover and refrigerate for about 6 hours or overnight until the custard sets.

Turn out onto a serving plate, top with extra raspberries, dust with icing sugar and serve with whipped cream on the side.

· 2 × vanilla and jam Swiss rolls
· 100ml dark rum
· Pulp from 8–10 passion fruits
· 150g raspberries, plus extra to serve
· Icing sugar, for dusting
· Whipped cream, to serve

FOR THE CUSTARD
· 500ml milk
· 400ml double cream
· 1 vanilla bean, split and seeds scraped
· 240g egg yolks
· 100g caster sugar
· 4 gelatine leaves
· 100g white chocolate, broken into pieces

RASPBERRY *and* ROSE QUEEN *of* PUDDINGS

Queen of Puddings is the most photogenic of desserts – a custard and jam base topped with a snowy white wig of meringue. Traditional ones are made with a base of breadcrumbs, but here I have created a custardy cake base that makes it all the more luxurious. Use a good natural rosewater – I especially like the Cortas brand which is commonly found in Middle Eastern shops – it has a delicate and subtle flavour unlike the brazen rose essences that taste chemical and harsh.

––––––––––

Preheat the oven to 170°C/Fan 150°C/Gas Mark 3½.

Separate your eggs and place the egg whites into a clean bowl. Place the egg yolks and caster sugar in a stand mixer and beat until they have combined and are light and fluffy. With the mixer still going on a low speed, gradually add the melted butter, vanilla extract and lemon zest. Fold in the flour – a third at a time. Gradually pour in the lukewarm milk and continue to beat on a low-medium speed to combine all of the ingredients.

Beat the egg whites with an electric whisk till you have stiff peaks and then gently fold into the cake batter. Pour the batter into a 20cm round pie dish and place into your preheated oven and cook for 30–35 minutes until it is golden but still has a gentle wobble. Set aside.

In the meantime, warm the jam in a pan along with the lemon juice to loosen up and then take off the heat and stir in the rosewater and raspberries. Set aside while you make the meringue.

Whisk the egg whites till they form firm peaks, then gradually whisk in the caster sugar till you have a thick and shiny meringue. Gently smooth the jam over the surface of the cake and then top with the meringue – this can be piped but I personally like to pile it up with a spoon and create a quiff or a dramatic peak. Put the dish back in the oven and bake for about 15 minutes till it is beautifully bronzed and serve.

· 4 eggs
· 175g caster sugar
· 125g butter, melted
· 1 tsp vanilla extract
· Zest of 1 lemon
· 100g plain flour
· 500ml lukewarm milk
· 200g raspberry jam
· 1 tbsp lemon juice
· 1 tbsp rosewater
· 250g raspberries

FOR THE MERINGUE
· 4 egg whites
· 125g caster sugar

INDEX

265

roulade, spiced apple and blackberry meringue 342–3

rum
- mango-misu 240
- upside-down white chocolate, raspberry and passion fruit pudding 256
- vegan piña colada trifle with tapioca custard 246–7

S

saag: Punjabi shalgam saag with chilli brown butter 164

saffron
- iles flottant with saffron and cardamom custard and pistachio caramel 236
- pea kofta scotch eggs with saffron yoghurt 44–6
- saffron, cauliflower and macaroni bake 144
- saffron malpuas with no-churn pistachio cream 80
- saffron sheermal 62
- saffron syrup 80
- spiced honey and saffron butter 228–9

salads
- charred melon and tomato panzanella 196
- cucumber chaat with labne 194
- grilled peaches with silken tofu and Thai basil and lime leaf gremolata 192
- heritage tomato salad with lime leaf dressing, ginger and chilli 190
- pea shoot salad 160–2
- roasted beetroot and blood orange salad with curry leaf dressing 195
- roasted carrot and hazelnut salad with freekeh, dates and orange blossom water 124
- watermelon salad with pepper and cashew-nut brittle 186

salsas
- kimchi, apple and pear salsa 208
- radish salsa 19

sambhar
- sambhar masala 98–101
- tamarind sambhar with semolina and coconut upma dumplings 98–101

savoiardi biscuits: mango-misu 240

schnitzels: Jerusalem artichoke and carrot schnitzel katsu curry 160–2

Scotch eggs, pea kofta 44–6

semolina and coconut upma dumplings 98–101

sesame seeds
- furukake 226
- Gujarati-style cavolo nero and chickpea flour rotolo with sesame seeds 200
- sesame tofu toasts 52

shaamba pickles 220

shallots, green lentil hummus with crisp 35

sheep's yoghurt: cold cucumber and sheep's yoghurt soup 90

sheermal, saffron 62

shiro miso udon mushroom and kale carbonara 146

shorba: sweetcorn and coconut shorba with popcorn and cashew clusters 108–9

soba noodles with cabbage, Brussels sprouts and almond butter dressing 153

sorrel, paneer braised in kale, spinach and 172

soups
- cacio e pepe chickpea, orzo and kale soup 112
- cauliflower soup with curried brown butter and Gruyere croutons 110
- cold cucumber and sheep's yoghurt soup 90
- hot & sour tomato soup with Thai basil oil and crispy noodles 102
- sweetcorn and coconut shorba with popcorn and cashew clusters 108–9

South Indian beetroot and coconut dip 20

spiced apple and blackberry meringue roulade 342–3

spiced honey and saffron butter 228–9

spicy cauliflower cheese parathas 82–3

spinach
- broccoli, kale and spinach kataifi pie 199
- green goddess dhal with preserved lemon 92
- paneer braised in kale, spinach and sorrel 172
- spinach and mung bean cheelas with avocado chutney and sprouts 79
- vegan courgette and spinach kofta makhani 179–80
- veggie breakfast bread and butter pudding 74–5

split pigeon peas: tamarind sambhar with semolina and coconut upma dumplings 98–101

squash
- lasagna of roasted squash, kale and walnuts 138
- squash and onion bhajis 104–5

strawberry falooda milk cake 244

sweet and sour dhal with chickpea flour pasta rags 148

sweet and sour stuffed okra fry 178

sweetcorn
- hot & sour sweetcorn risotto with lime leaf butter 125
- hot cheese and corn dip with jalapeno relish 26
- sweetcorn and coconut shorba with popcorn and cashew clusters 108–9
- sweetcorn, lemongrass and lime leaf fritters 50

Swiss rolls: upside-down white chocolate, raspberry and passion fruit pudding 256

T

tahini
- Beiruti jewelled noodle rice with tahini sauce 120
- pasta fatteh with tahini yoghurt and caramelised onions 142

tamarind
- braised pumpkin with tamarind, cashew nuts and coconut 174
- date and tamarind chutney 226
- tamarind and tomato chutney 47
- tamarind sambhar with semolina and coconut upma dumplings 98–101

tapioca custard 246–7

Thai basil
- grilled peaches with silken tofu and Thai basil and lime leaf gremolata 192

U

V

W

Y

269

Z

ACKNOWLEDGEMENTS

First and foremost – thank you to you dearest readers for your support. It is such a privilege to imagine that this book might be on your bookshelves or in your kitchen – that some of these recipes might bring you and your loved ones together around a table.

Thank you, Rowan Yapp, for your dedication to *Comfort and Joy*, for championing it when it was only a fragile dream. Thank you for believing in my vision for the book and for drawing together a constellation of stars to bring it to life.

Felicity Blunt – I am so lucky to have your endless support, wisdom and friendship. Thank you for always passionately advocating for my ideas and for being the gourmand you are – you remain one of my very favourite people to cook for. Thank you Sabhbh Curran for being a trusted confidante, for shepherding me through the whole process of this book. I really admire your wit, kindness and brilliant mind – you are my platonic work crush.

Kristin Perers, Tabitha Hawkins and Joss Herd – the remarkable three. Thank you for making me feel so held and enveloped in joy on our days together at the beautiful Flower Factory Studio. Kristin, I have such admiration for your creative spirit, your ability to see beauty and poetry in even the most inane, the way the light wondrously bends to your vision, your resoluteness and unwillingness to compromise even when you are acrobatically balanced on the top rung of the most precarious step ladder.

Tabitha – only you are dedicated enough to mount the most fragile trifle bowl onto your bicycle and pedal across London. What an honour and a pleasure it is to be immersed in your shimmering magic and the wonder-smitten worlds you create. I am in awe of your undiminishing energy. Your feeling for life, your warmth and excitement always nourishes me.

Joss – no one can articulate the flavours in my recipes better than you. Thank you for your generous wholehearted devotion to this book. You create euphoric clouds of meringue, swirl patterns of icing, chop onions and juggle pots and pans all while dancing to the rhythmic whirr of a stand mixer – I'll never know how you do it all, but I am full of the deepest gratitude.

Hattie Arnold, you are vastly talented, industrious and yet so humble – a balm amongst the immense complexity of a multitude of recipes all being prepared at the same time. Thank you for agreeing to be part of this.

Thank you also to Aloha Shaw for lending your talent, for your enthusiasm, sweet nature and attention to detail.

Sandra Zellmer – how lucky I am to have made two books with you now. Thank you for your amazing capability of taking what was unsaid in my heart and making it a physical thing. Your design is so thoughtful and elegant – always giving readers space to think and even dream.

Laura Nickoll – thank you for your empathetic nature. Anytime I felt overwhelmed you provided a clever structure for clarifying and organising so I could have ample space and time for thinking, reflecting and decision making. You have been an invaluable support. Thank you especially for your tenderness with my words.

Laura Creyke, Fran Owen, Mari Yamazaki – I am so privileged to have such a triumph of a team to shout about the book. Thank you for your enthusiasm and creativity – for taking the time to get to know me and working with me so collaboratively. Thank you for thinking unconventionally and giving me opportunities to do things differently.

Gemma Bell – you are the bestest in the biz and life. Your agile efforts and knack for communicating mine and Jikoni's story are unmatched. I have enormous respect for your dynamism and hustle. Thanks for being the kindest friend and professional cheerleader. Also shouting out Lois Brown, Alicia Fellowes and Chloe Desrosches – the smartest (and most fun) team who aren't afraid of rolling up their sleeves.

Jay Rayner – thank you for all the words of wisdom and being my mentor. Thank you for your generosity, advice and being an emotional ballast in the hard times. I owe you a lot and probably wouldn't have had the confidence to enter the playground without knowing you were there watching over me from the gates.

Al Gilmour, Tim Lusher and Mina Holland – friends and talented editors. Al, thank you for teaching me be spare with my words and for keeping me on my toes. Tim and Mina – writing for you at Feast is a food writer's dream. Thank you for giving me an opportunity that allows me to develop both as a writer and a cook.

Diana Henry and Roopa Gulati. I love you both. Your kindness and advice and those long dinners together have meant more to me than you know. It means so much to me to have the love and support of two food writers and cooks I look up to so much.

Thank you to Caleb Azumah Nelson, Diana Henry, Anita Rani, Claudia Roden, Meera Syal and Sathnam Sanghera for your kind words. You are all so gracious. I have such admiration not just for the pioneering work you do in your fields, but the path you have built for the next generation.

Aisha Gill – thank you for the friendship and sisterhood. You are uncommonly courageous. Your ability to stand against life's ugly injustices and yet still see the world as a garden of endless optimism and delight astounds me. I am always learning from you.

Sham Sandhu, my brother. Spending time with you is always like walking through a lush garden – healing. I am in awe of your soulful intelligence and your astute knack for bringing good people together. Thank you for your care and thoughtfulness.

Neel Kapur and Rhys Baker – I am fortunate to have you as my extended family. Your inimitable hospitality means that not just our guests, but our whole team feels the special brand of magic, comfort and joy you have helped to create. Neel, your unflappability and ability to juggle the restaurant's many moving parts keeps us on our toes – thank you. Thank you also to all the genial team at Jikoni for your constant dedication and hard work.

Thank you, Rosa Safiah Connell, for intuitively curating clothes and accessories that were just perfect for the openers including many from my favourites Alemais, Alighieri, By Rotation, Rejina Pyo. Thank you for your generous support and friendship – Rosh Mahtani, Eshita Kabra, Daisy Hoppen and the team at DHPR. Zac Campbell-Muir – thank you for weaving braids and magic with your make-up brushes. Thank you also Sage Appliances and Amara.com for providing kitchen and prop support.

Thank you, Gabriella Khalil and the whole team, at the stunning Palm Heights Grand Cayman for your generous hospitality as I put the finishing touches to my manuscript. A desk in paradise certainly increased my productivity.

My love Nadeem. Everything I thought I knew about love before I met you seems pretty absurd now. Thank you for opening the windows and doors of my heart and letting the light in. Your infinite goodness and grace inspire me every day and I feel very lucky that you are mine.

Moaz and Shany Nanjuwany – thank you for making me part of your family. You have always focused your lives on establishing meaningful goals and having a positive impact on others. Thank you for always listening, for encouraging us and being present – I love you both dearly.

ABOUT THE AUTHOR

Born in Kenya to Indian parents, Ravinder Bhogal's food is inspired by her own mixed heritage and the UK's diverse immigrant culture. Ravinder is a journalist, chef and restaurateur. Her restaurant, Jikoni, was ranked 56th in the UK by the National Restaurant Awards within 7 months of opening and achieved a coveted place in the Michelin Guide in the same year. It is the UK's first independent restaurant to go carbon-neutral. In June 2020, during the pandemic, Ravinder launched a sustainable vegetarian home delivery brand, Comfort and Joy, as a sister brand to Jikoni.

She has authored two books. *Jikoni: Proudly Inauthentic Recipes from an Immigrant Kitchen* (Bloomsbury, 2020), was winner of the IACP Awards Best Chef/ Restaurant Cookbook and was shortlisted for both the André Simon Award and Fortnum & Mason's Food and Drink Awards. Her debut book, *Cook in Boots* (HarperCollins, 2009), won the Gourmand World Cookbook Award for the UK's Best First Cookbook and was awarded the first runner-up's prize for the World's Best First Cookbook at the Paris Cookbook Fair in February 2010.

She is a food columnist for the *FT Weekend Magazine* and *Guardian Feast,* a contributing editor at *Harper's Bazaar,* and regularly writes for publications such as the *Observer Magazine, Waitrose Food Magazine, Delicious Magazine* and *Vogue* online.

Ravinder has travelled the globe as roving reporter for Channel 4's magazine show Food: What Goes in your Basket? and has also presented a special two-part documentary The Great British Curry Trail for BBC2. She has also appeared on Radio 4's Woman's Hour, Channel 4's Sunday Brunch, BBC1's Saturday Kitchen and Masterchef and ITV's Saturday Morning with James Martin and This Morning. She has been seen on primetime Indian television with her own 22-part series, Ravinder's Kitchen (BBC Worldwide), which has been sold across Asia and the Middle East. Ravinder has twice been named in the Evening Standard Progress 1000 as one of London's leading influencers of progress and diversity in the capital. Code Hospitality named her one of the most influential women in food three times.

Ravinder can be found documenting her adventures in food on her Instagram page: @cookinboots